# Straight Out of The Trailer Park

How Mindset and Perseverance Enabled One Man to Overcome His Poor White Trash Upbringing and Live a Fulfilling Life

Loyd Hawkins

# Dedication

This book is dedicated to my wife, Donna, without whom I would never have become the man I am. She has supported me without reservation and has followed me across the globe over our 35+ year marriage. From Florida to Alaska and everywhere in between, she has been my rock! Thank you, SHUG, for all you have given me and our family.

# Acknowledgment

I would like to extend a personal Thank You to people who have made a great impact on my life.

**Nedla Gonzy** – I will never forget your selfless kindness.

**Jon Stevens** – Mentor and Friend. Thank you, Jon, for your guidance, friendship, and insights.

**Mike Cowles** – Mentor and Friend. Thank you, Mike, for your overwatch, humor, friendship, and insights

**David Johnston** – Mentor and Friend. One of my best friends and my professional rock! You are the best!

**Braden Prickett** – Consigliari and Friend. Always there for me and always willing to challenge! I love you, buddy.

**Felipe Neto** – BJJ Professor and Friend. Always willing to give all of himself to his students, I would not have achieved my black belt. Additionally, without Felipe, I would have never been exposed to so many wonderful friends.

And lastly, **Captain BobbyAllen,** who told me to "Stop bitching about Commissioned Officers and change my life, or SHUT UP." This was my first exposure to taking ownership of my life and changing my mindset

# Table of Contents

# About the Author

Growing up in poverty as the only child of a single mother, Loyd had the odds stacked against him. With no father figure or strong male role model, Loyd was forced to figure out life on his own. Fortune smiled upon him when he made the decision to join the US Army. During his time in the Army, he flourished, serving in a variety of roles, most notably as a paratrooper in the 5th Special Forces Group (A) and the renowned 101st Airborne Division. It was here that Loyd received a graduate-level education in leadership.

After leaving the Army, Loyd sought his next challenge by enrolling in graduate school at Florida State University. There, he earned his MBA and promptly joined the esteemed global consulting firm Accenture. During his tenure at Accenture and other consulting practices, he cultivated a deep understanding of sales, delivery, small and large team building, as well as interpersonal relationships and communication.

"Never satisfied" is the best phrase to aptly characterize Loyd's mindset. Whether achieving his black belt in Brazilian Jiu-Jitsu or participating in the 'Escape from Alcatraz' swim, Loyd constantly seeks personal growth. Scuba diving and skydiving are also among his cherished passions.

Loyd aspires to wring the most out of life and hopes to share his passion and perspective with you, inspiring you to lead your best life.

# Chapter 1: Where It All Started

The sun's fading rays painted the park in hues of orange, casting long shadows that danced with a forlorn grace. It was in this park, where innocence and darkness coexisted that an unforgettable scene unfolded - one that has etched itself deep into my memory as a child.

As a child, the world can be a mystifying place, full of wonder and excitement. But for my sister and me, childhood was tinged with a sorrowful undertone.

On that evening, my sister and I were standing, captivated, on the other side of a worn wrought iron fence, our tiny hands clutching its cold bars. There, sprawled upon a wooden bench, lay my father, unconscious and vulnerable. His battered body was proof of the storm raging within our home. Hovering above him was our mother. Her fury knew no bounds in that moment, and she was expressing her pent-up rage on our father, who was lying motionless.

My sister and I were witnessing this agonizing sight as the fragility of our family lay bare before us. My young heart trembled, consumed by a profound mixture of terror, anger, and helplessness. As the vicious blows rained down on my father's motionless form, a desperate impulse welled up within me.

Turning to my sister, I whispered, *"I will cut my dad with the can opener I found in the dirt."*

Little did I know then, standing on the precipice of that life-altering scene, that this would be the catalyst for the unwritten chapters of my life. That the clash of brokenness and survival would set the stage for a life shaped by hardship, endurance, and, ultimately, triumph. And that… I would break free from the shackles of my past and emerge as a survivor, not a victim.

If only that little man standing behind the fence knew…

\*\*\*

I took my first breath on a chilly winter night in the heart of Chicago, a city renowned for its resilience and staunch spirit. The year was 1966, which was a time of shifting societal norms and an evolving world.

In the backdrop of a bustling metropolis, my family existed on the margins of society. My mother had come from humble beginnings in the hills of West Virginia and only reached the high school level of education. In those times, this only equipped my mom to serve as a secretary or other low-level positions, with ZERO upward mobility. On the other hand, my father was a roofer and carried his own burdens, haunted by the demons that drove him to seek solace in alcohol. His addiction cast a shadow over our family, its reach extending far beyond the physical walls of our home.

I remember I was merely three or four years old, perched on a weathered curb in the bustling streets of Chicago. My father came and sat beside me. He was clutching a small bottle in his weathered hands, filled with a translucent liquid that he claimed was nothing more than water. He tried to give it to me and asked me to drink it.

Curious, I reached out to accept the offering, but as I brought the bottle closer, the pungent scent of alcohol pierced through the charade, shattering the illusion he had crafted. In my childlike wisdom, I knew something was amiss, so I refused to drink it. I didn't know it then, but it was Vodka he was offering to his 3-year-old boy.

If I talk about my mother's journey, her story began in 1944. She was born in the rugged landscapes of Appalachia into a world marked by scarcity and limited opportunities. The tragedy cast its dark shadow over her life at a tender age. At just nine years old, she was orphaned by her mother, snatched away by the merciless grip of cervical cancer. The year was the early 1950s, a time when healthcare was a far cry from the advanced systems we have today, especially in the poorest regions of Appalachia.

Growing up in the poorest corners of Appalachia, my mother witnessed firsthand the stark disparities that cast a long shadow over her formative years. Abandoned by her two older brothers and her father, she found herself navigating the harsh landscapes of life without the pillars of family to lean on. Instead, she was entrusted to the care of a couple whose religious fervor masked their capacity for empathy and acceptance. They were devout Baptists, their beliefs steeped in fire and brimstone, their tongues laden with judgment and condemnation.

Within the walls of that sheltered existence, my mother was subjected to relentless beratement and emotional turmoil. Instead of finding the nurturing love she so desperately craved, she was met with constant criticism that made her feel inadequate and unworthy. The echoes of their disapproval seeped into the very fabric of her being, shaping her self-perception and leaving invisible scars that lingered for years.

Yearning to break free from the suffocating grip of her oppressive environment, she seized an opportunity for escape at the age of 18. She ventured into the unknown, stepping into a world that held both promise and uncertainty. In her quest for liberation, she found herself entangled in a relationship with an older man, which resulted in the birth of my older sister. Seeking a fresh start, she was drawn to a city teeming with possibilities and a chance for redemption - Chicago. Thus, she relocated, and it was here that she came across my father, married him, and I found my place in the world.

As you would peel back the layers of my story, you will realize that my childhood was far from ideal. In the confines of our home, my mother's frustration and desperation manifested in acts of violence, which resulted in her being very abusive. Uneducated and burdened by the weight of providing for our family, she resorted to using anything within her reach as a weapon to discipline me. Hair brushes, coat hangers, you name it, and that turned into an instrument of pain. Each strike, though borne out of her own struggles and the absence of guidance, left indelible marks upon my heart and body.

Reflecting upon those tumultuous years, I have come to understand the complexities of my mother's actions. In a world devoid of support systems, devoid of the resources needed to navigate life's challenges, she was trapped in a cycle of despair and survival. Her actions were borne out of a desperate belief that what she was doing was somehow in the best interest of her children. In acknowledging the circumstances that shaped her, I have learned to untangle the knots of resentment and blame. I recognize that the absence of a support system, coupled with her own unmet needs and unhealed wounds, played a pivotal role in the cycle of abuse.

Nonetheless, I cannot deny the absence of solid guidance and advice in navigating the path to manhood. My mother gave me no solid young man advice, which makes the absence of guidance and mentorship from a father figure starkly apparent. My mother was burdened by the weight of raising three children on a meager waitress salary. She was faced with the arduous task of navigating the complexities of life without the presence of a solid male role model.

It is true that the absence of a male role model during my formative years created a void - a void that left me yearning for direction, mentorship, and a blueprint for navigating the complexities of masculinity. The lack of a father figure meant that I had to piece together my understanding of manhood from the fragments of experiences and the influences that surrounded me.

Growing up in the throes of extreme poverty, the lessons I learned were often born out of necessity. I witnessed firsthand the strength, resilience, and resourcefulness of my mother as she fought tooth and nail to provide for our family. While it is natural to wonder how different things might have been had I received more direct guidance from a father figure, I have come to accept that life unfolds in ways beyond our control.

# Chapter 2: "Shut Up" and Unheard

Among the myriad memories that linger from my formative years, one remains crystal clear even to this day - a memory that embodies the complexities of navigating poverty within the confines of the educational system. I recall receiving a food basket from the local middle school because I was one of the poorest kids. I was grappled with a range of emotions - embarrassment, vulnerability, and even a tinge of shame.

Throughout the entirety of my childhood and into adulthood, I grew up in a trailer park, where having a room, let alone a bed to sleep in, was nothing but a distant dream. The trailer park was our dwelling, a place where I learned to adapt to limited space and resources. While my peers may have had their rooms and comfortable beds, I made the best of what I had, spending most of my childhood up to adulthood sleeping on a couch.

As a child, I often found myself lost in daydreams about meeting my older brother, but we'll talk about him and all his adventures later. I was just a young man fantasizing about having a better life. These daydreams were a source of inspiration during moments of difficulty or when the reality of my circumstances seemed overwhelming.

With the winds of change blowing in our direction, we moved to Tennessee when my mother crossed paths with a man named Bill Hannah in Chicago, likely in a bar. Bill hailed from the hills of Tennessee, and that's where life took us next. Despite this change in location and the addition of a second adult figure in our lives, we continued to face financial struggles and continued to remain in the grips of poverty. Sadly, this period was marked by an even darker aspect - Bill's behavior was extremely abusive.

Living in Tennessee brought about new challenges, and despite the presence of two adults in our household, the financial situation didn't improve. Instead, it became increasingly difficult due to Bill's abusive nature. The burden of poverty was worsened by the fear and pain caused by Bill's abusive actions. The place that was supposed to offer us a fresh start became entangled in a web of distress and heartache.

When I was in third grade, I decided to enjoy myself. It was a day when my curious spirit led me to venture home with a friend without notifying my mom or stepdad. I hadn't thought through the consequences of my actions - I was just caught up in the adventure. However, fate had other plans.

When my mom and stepdad found out what I had done, their worry turned to fear, and fear gave way to sheer anger. At last, when I was in front of them, I knew I had made a grave mistake. Before I could explain, their emotions erupted like a volcanic eruption. Without any warning, Bill grabbed his belt from a nearby chair. My heart pounded faster than ever as I saw the fury in his eyes.

The belt came crashing down on my young back, and I winced in pain. Blow after blow, I could barely comprehend what was happening. The stinging sensation mixed with the emotional turmoil dazed me. As the beating continued, I couldn't hold back my tears. I felt not only physical pain but also a deep emotional wound with every strike. When it finally ended, I could barely stand. My legs trembled, and sitting down seemed like an impossible task.

Among the various instances of abuse that I witnessed, one remains etched into my memory. I remember I was holding a bull's horn in my hands (this type of object was decorative in nature and really served no functional purpose) and noticed its shiny surface. Without a second thought, I brought it close to my lips and blew into it, producing a sound that rang through the air. But little did I know that someone was watching from a distance – Bill. In what seemed like an instant, Bill was standing before me, his face contorted with anger. Before I could react, he snatched the horn from my hands with such force that it startled me. But that wasn't the end of it.

In a moment of uncontrollable rage, he swung the horn back. The sharp edge of the horn collided with my mouth, causing searing pain as it cut my lip and left my nose bleeding. Shocked and hurt, I took a step back with tears streaming down my face. As the pain radiated through my tiny body, I struggled to comprehend why this had happened. But it was no surprise that he was an alcoholic as well.

My mother had reached a breaking point after this incident. She knew it was time to escape the toxic environment we were in, so she made a courageous decision - we ran off to Florida, seeking a fresh start and leaving behind the painful memories of our past.

Florida became our new home, and I was raised there from the age of 11 onwards. It was a place of unfamiliarity, but we reconnected with my grandfather, the same man who had once abandoned my mother. There was a tenuousness in our relationship, knowing that wounds from the past still lingered, not to forget that they didn't help us at all.

Growing up in North Florida wasn't easy either. Despite the move being a fresh start, it wasn't the haven we had hoped for. Struggling fiscally, we faced numerous challenges, and the people who were supposed to provide support and help didn't step up to the plate. As a poor redneck kid, life was filled with adversities and limitations. With an older sister and a much younger one (9 years my junior), our days were spent navigating the trials of life, particularly when it came to our mother's unpredictable schedule. She often left her work at odd hours of the night and during the day, leaving my siblings and me to fend for ourselves. The absence of parental guidance created a void in our lives, forcing us to rely on our own devices to navigate the world.

During those years, we became self-reliant at an early age. Each morning, my siblings and I would wake up early, making our own breakfast before heading off to school. Upon our return, we would prepare our dinner and complete our homework. We were pretty much self-raised.

As kids with almost no parental presence, we sometimes found ourselves getting into mischief, roaming freely in the neighborhood without a sense of boundaries. My older sister and I often returned home from school without any supervision. Being left unattended was a routine we had grown accustomed to, but little did we know that it would soon attract the attention of others in our trailer park community. Concerned parents, noticing our lack of adult supervision, reached out to Child Protective Services, thinking we might have been abandoned.

It was a moment that would change the dynamics of our family forever. When my mother learned of the intervention, she reacted by placing us on an unexpected "home arrest" of sorts. Thus, my sister and I found ourselves confined within the boundaries of our tiny trailer until our mother returned home each day.

One memory that remains vivid is when I resorted to shoplifting Kool-Aid and other food just to ensure we had something to eat. Life had dealt us a difficult hand, but we managed to survive by relying on our own resourcefulness.

An incident from my 8th-grade year stands out prominently. As part of the library staff, we were granted the opportunity to enjoy a picnic at Tom Brown Park. Excitement filled the air as everyone gave their money to the teachers, who were going to fetch food from McDonald's. I found myself in an unfortunate position, unable to contribute anything due to our financial struggles. While my peers enjoyed their meals, I was the only one with a humble fried egg sandwich. I felt embarrassed and isolated.

I also recall the Christmas when my family received a food box from my school. This box, brimming with donated food, was a lifeline for the poorest of the poor families during the holiday season. My only respite of this entire childhood was the fact that I loved to read 'Field and Stream' and 'Outdoor Life' magazines. These publications became my gateway to worlds I had never experienced, captivating my imagination in ways I couldn't have imagined. Each page opened up a whole new realm of adventure and possibility, providing me with an escape from the hardships of reality.

I became engrossed in every line, devouring every page with an insatiable appetite for knowledge. With each magazine, my vocabulary expanded exponentially. I soaked up new words, phrases, and concepts, enriching my language skills beyond what was typical for a child my age. Within the power of these printed words, I found affirmation of my dreams - a validation that there was more to life than what I was experiencing. I knew that I was destined for more than living in a trailer park.

Throughout my life, there's one phrase I've heard repeatedly more than anything: "Shut up!" Time and again, this phrase became a disheartening chorus, stifling the voice that yearned to be heard. People failed to recognize or nurture the gift I possessed - the ability to connect with others in a genuine and authentic way. I have a unique talent for reaching out to people and a natural ability to empathize, listen, and genuinely understand others' emotions and experiences. But this gift was overlooked, overshadowed by the weight of those two hurtful words.

# Chapter 3: High School Tales

Picture this: the years were 1980 to 1982 - no internet, just the faint whisper of cable TV. Back then, the girls were a work of art, untouched by filters and so stunningly genuine.

Now, let me transport you to a sprawling parking lot, the pre-school hangout spot. We converged there, a tribe of teenagers, before the first bell rang or during the lunchtime hustle. And oh, the vehicles! Pickup trucks proudly bore rifle or shotgun racks, a sight that would raise eyebrows today but was the norm back then.

My stomping ground was Amos P Godby High School, home of the fierce "Cougars," nestled in none other than the charming Tallahassee, Florida. It's where memories were etched, friendships were forged, and life's adventures were scribbled in the yearbook of time.

Stepping through those doors was like entering a time capsule, transporting me straight into the heart of the vibrant 80s. Amidst the corridors that seemed to stretch into eternity and the inviting open breezeways stood my unassuming high school - a place that could easily make a 14-year-old freshman feel like a mere speck in a giant maze. It was very intimidating, to say the least.

As you can imagine, the land of lockers and lectures, where the difference between a 14-year-old still navigating the world of pimples and voice cracks and a 17-year-old who had triumphantly sailed through puberty, was as glaring as the noonday sun. As fate would have it, I became a frequent flyer in the boxing ring of high school life. Why, you ask? Because I had a knack for standing tall even when bullies cast long shadows.

In the grand fashion show of high school, I sported a wardrobe that could be counted on one hand, which was a testament to the tight grip of poverty. And popularity, well, let's just say I was more of a hidden gem, waiting to be discovered amidst the glitter and glamour. Little did I know, my world was devoid of a spectrum that others saw vividly. It wasn't until I enlisted in the Army in 1984 that the truth hit me - I was color blind. All those years, from the classroom to the hallway, I was blissfully unaware of the invisible rainbow I couldn't see. My fashion choices were a symphony of mismatched notes that drew more than a few chuckles. Yet, I pretty much just ignored the critics. And, as luck would have it, there was no guiding maternal compass to steer me through the sea of hues and shades.

But here's the twist: despite my fashion escapades, my personality was a kaleidoscope of intrigue. Like a magnet for laughter, I found myself at the center of orbits. My humor, sharp as a tailor's needle, stitched bonds that people couldn't resist. I was the walking embodiment of a punchline, my quips and jests proving irresistible to those around me. Confidence coursed through my veins, which was a quality I brandished with the finesse of a seasoned warrior, even though its origins remained a mystery. Call it wit, call it smarts, or perhaps just a pinch of plain old audacity - these ingredients brewed a concoction that had everyone under its spell. So, there I stood, navigating a world of mismatched shirts and colorblind confusion, armed with a personality that could light up a room even in the darkest of colorless corners.

People always told me I was funny. But it was in the hallowed halls of my 9th-grade civics class that a different kind of chuckle echoed. I had asked a seemingly outlandish question: what if we multiplied human speed by the rotational speed of the earth? The class erupted in laughter, but amidst the amusement, a surprising validation surfaced. Mr. Cooper, our teacher and custodian of knowledge, decided to cast a spotlight on my query. With a knowing smile, he shared a gem that resonated deeper than the laughter. "This is a similar question," he declared, "that once graced the thoughts of none other than Einstein himself during the birthing process of his theory of general relativity." Cue the mic drop moment.

In that instant, my quip became a quasar of intellect, shining far brighter than a mere jest. This revelation left me feeling incredibly good. On a side note, Mr. Steve Cooper was a very kind and assuring teacher; he was my favorite.

I used to chill with some brainy, nerdy pals, which surprisingly turned me into the de facto leader of our crew and gave my leadership skills a boost. My buddy, Steve Reecy, was a year ahead of me in school and one year older. We spent a ton of time together, and he had this knack for acting like the Einstein of the group (especially acting like he was smarter than me.) Oddly enough, his genius act lit a fire under me, pushing me to put in some serious effort. Eventually, I transformed into a guy that Steve and others secretly wished they could be.

Back in the day, I was your typical "meh" student who barely put in any effort. Despite that, I somehow managed to snag decent grades (except for math, where I hit a roadblock) thanks to my pretty sharp memory. This memory superpower had a cool side effect - I ended up being a regular chatterbox in class. But all that talking gave me a real boost of confidence when it came to addressing a bunch of people at once.

If I could spin a tale of being a ladies' man, that would be a stretch. Reality check: I was far from it. I stumbled through a couple of brief flings with girls who probably took pity on me or found my faux confidence intriguing. Unfortunately, my lack of riches and resources seriously shrunk my dating prospects. I mingled with a few girls from my trailer park, but it wasn't exactly a fairy tale romance.

My crew of pals, who were all a notch better off than me, formed a tight-knit squad I rolled with. Being both penniless and on the scrawnier side, plus the absence of a father figure meant I often missed those subtle moments when girls were throwing out flirts. Yet, I did have a couple of really sweet girlfriends who brought a lot of niceness into my life (Kudos to Kathy Scott!).

One memory that's etched in my mind hails from my 7th-grade days. We had to endure these mandatory Square Dancing classes, where we had to pair up with someone of the opposite gender. I casually sauntered over to a girl I'd known for ages, Krystal Braden, and told her, "Hey Krystal, I'll dance with you!"

Her response? A swift "Oh no, you won't!" followed by a hasty exit. Honestly, I thought she'd be up for it since we were pals. Years later, she revealed that if she'd known how things would pan out for me in high school, she'd have gladly danced with me. These were the social queues that I missed.

Another one of the most prominent things during my high school days was my height. High school kicked off for me in 9th grade, standing at a solid 5 foot 5. Then, out of the blue in my sophomore year, I shot up to a towering 6 foot 3. Suddenly, the spotlight was on – girls were giving me the nod, and some guys, possibly feeling a tad uneasy about my self-assuredness or possibly threatened by my confidence, started taking notice, too.

However, let's cut to the chase – the real thorn in my dating journey was, you guessed it, my lack of funds. No wheels, no cash, and no job in my corner. Trust me, trying to win hearts gets pretty darn challenging when you're juggling empty pockets and an absence of transportation! This makes it really hard to court women!

I've got this crystal-clear memory from my graphic arts class. The teacher really wasn't my biggest fan. Can't blame him; I was a non-stop chatterbox and a world-class tease to boot.

Picture this: I was seated right behind a senior classman, a strapping football player who had caught the affection of a sophomore girl from our shared past. Now, I was a sophomore too, always ready with a wisecrack to liven up the class. In the grand tradition of mischief, I couldn't resist the urge to pepper the class with my clever quips. Of course, the teacher wasn't amused and had developed an aversion to my constant verbal acrobatics and the amusement I spread. Also, I might have taken a few jabs at Mr. Football along the way. It was he who became the target of my verbal antics. I wasn't too keen on his romantic escapades with a 15-year-old sophomore, and my comedic artillery was locked and loaded against him.

But here's where the tale takes a twist. One fine day, our gridiron hero had had enough. He spun around, grabbed me by the neck with both his hands, and unleashed a volcanic "WILL YOU SHUT THE F**K UP?!"

Now, what happened next is like a scene from a sitcom. My brain, as it often does in moments of chaos, conjured a retort of epic proportions. With a squeeze on my vocal cords, a squeaky voice escaped in a high-pitched voice, "What are you gonna do, kiss me?"

That's when the class exploded into laughter. The poor guy turned beet red with embarrassment and let go of my neck, which was getting a little too friendly with his grip. As you might expect, the teacher stayed out of it. He was probably secretly rooting for a show; he might have furtively wanted to see me get my ass kicked. Lesson learned: sometimes, just sometimes, silence is golden. But again, this was another episode where I just should have shut up. But well, at least I scored a hilarious memory out of it!

At the end of the day, I would just say, *Hang in there* because life's got a way of turning up the brightness. Dark days play a part, but they're just a prelude to the brilliance that follows. The shadows are just setting the stage for the spotlight. Back in high school, if you'd asked around, you'd have been met with skeptical glances and shrugged shoulders. The naysayers would have bet against me, casting their doubts like shadows on my path. If the rumor mill had its say, my success story might've sounded like fiction. But armed with tenacity, perseverance, and a sprinkle of luck, I stand today as the headliner in my graduation tale and can confidently and proudly state that I am the most accomplished person in my graduating class.

So, remember, when the clouds gather, and the world seems like a daunting labyrinth, take a deep breath and hold tight. For beyond the storm, a dawn of opportunities awaits. And I stand here as a living testament, assuring you that the journey is worth it. Hang in there, my friend - life's grand picture has remarkable things in store for you.

# Chapter 4: A Costly Choice

High school is the phase of life that comprises defining moments that shape the very clay of our character. The same is the case with me. Among the vivid memories, a few stand tall like monuments of transformation. First and foremost, which now you already know, there was the growth spurt that felt like Mother Nature's turbo boost. From a mere 5 foot 5 to an impressive 6 foot 3 in a single calendar flip! Suddenly, I was catching the eyes of a certain crowd: the enchanting kingdom of the female gaze. Oh, the mysteries of attraction!

But that wasn't the only transformation. Like a butterfly emerging from its cocoon, I shed my indifference toward traditional education. It's safe to say that the conventional education scene lost its grip on me. It was as if my priorities realigned, like stars finding their place in the night sky. The classroom became a work of snores and sighs while life's practical lessons took center stage.

Then came the whole realm of physical confrontations - a rite of passage that can truly shape a young man's perception of himself. I crossed paths with a few folks in that arena, and guess what? These encounters wrapped a cloak of confidence around me. Confrontations became more than mere threats, which led me into several physical clashes and, ultimately, allowed me to gain confidence that I could defend myself. See, a bunch of kids, mostly guys with an extra dose of testosterone, might believe they've got the combat skills to back their talk. But when push comes to shove, not many step into the ring. I, on the other hand, didn't shy away from these confrontations. In a world where bravado is often just that - empty boasting - I walked the talk. In fact, I turned them into practice sessions, building up a real-world assurance in my ability to stand my ground.

So there you have it, the ingredients that stirred the cauldron of my adolescence - towering growth, a recalibrated focus, and a willingness to back words with action. These were the strokes that painted the canvas of my youth, and even now, they remain as vibrant brushstrokes in the grand masterpiece of my life.

The major thing about high school is that it's like this pivotal phase where, while you're deep in the midst of it, it feels like everything. Sure, back in those hallowed halls, every pop quiz felt like a life-or-death match, and that cafeteria chatter seemed to hold the secrets of the universe. However, it didn't take me long to see through. High school is just a mere stepping stone in the grand mosaic of life.

As the years grew in my rearview mirror, so did my understanding. Looking back, I realize it means nothing. It tugs at my heart for those who clutch onto their high school glory days, whether they wore the football team's captain badge or rocked the cheerleader's pompoms. You can spot them from a mile away – still anchored in the past, mentally stuck.

Me? I walked a different path - a winding one filled with bumps and detours. I was a so-so student, carrying a vault of untapped potential. Mediocre student, once-so-thin-I-could-bend-in-the-wind - these were my companions. And yes, my self-confidence took a few hits. But hindsight is the most powerful rearview mirror, and now it's clear as a crisp morning - I had allowed the illusion of high school to dwarf my self-worth.

High School is just a pebble on the vast shore of existence. The real journey - the one that truly shapes us - unfolds beyond its walls. As I look back, I shake my head with a knowing smile, realizing that I understood it even at that age, and now, I stand tall, knowing it's just a speck in the constellation of life's grand adventure.

High school unveiled two standout mentors who left their fingerprints on my journey. First in line is none other than the maestro of civics himself, Mr. Cooper. He had this uncanny knack for showing me that my smarts were worth their weight in gold. Mr. Cooper fashioned an oasis of support where all of us students could flourish. His classroom wasn't just a realm of lectures; it was a sanctuary of encouragement. A place where the timid blossomed and the eager thrived. He also frequently summoned me into discussions – it turns out I was quite participative in his class.

Next up, the spotlight shines on Coach Keel, the coach of our physical education. In stature, he might have been diminutive, but in spirit, he towered. His coaching sessions were like forging steel - the heat, the pressure, all tempered with unwavering fairness. Coach Keel was a man who appreciated the sweat equity, and as luck would have it, I was never short of it. My dedication to sweating it out in his class and my unending willingness to dive into activities caught his attention.

As my narrative has unfolded in these pages, there's one towering hurdle that loomed above all else in my journey: growing up steeped in poverty, devoid of any male role models except the two teachers I just mentioned. In those crucial years, I found myself standing at life's crossroads, equipped with an arsenal of dreams but lacking the crucial map to navigate the intricate pathways of human connection. It was like navigating a labyrinth without a map. Conversing with girls and smoothing out friend tiffs, my toolkit was limited to one option: violence. Imagine being this tall, scrawny six-foot-three kid, brimming with curiosity and interest in girls but crippled by a lack of know-how in approaching, dating, and projecting any semblance of achievement. The toll on my self-esteem? Let's just say it ran deep.

\*\*\*

As they say, *not all influence is good.*

Donnie Friday was a charismatic rogue who wove both allure and chaos into my life. Picture this: a friend who radiated an air of rebellion, one who whispered promises of a life far from the drudgery of the classroom.

Donnie was a vortex of influence, a force that both attracted and repelled. Older by a mere six months, he seemed to possess an enigmatic magnetism. He had this knack for being a not-so-great influence, yet there was something intriguing about him that I couldn't help but admire. A pocket-sized powerhouse, he strutted with an aura that screamed adventure, while I, towering in height, lacked the same confidence. Our paths diverged in physical stature, yet in rebellion, he stood as a towering colossus.

And so, influenced by his alluring talks and personality, *I quit high school.*

As for how my decision to quit high school was received by those around me – family, friends, and the like? Truth be told, it seemed like my choice didn't really register on their radar. During that phase, I also fell down the rabbit hole of smoking a fair bit of marijuana, which definitely didn't help matters. Donnie sold me on this fantasy that seemed like an endless summer, a never-ending loop of hunting, fishing, and bliss. But as they say, reality bites.

My bubble burst when my mother reminded me that a job was non-negotiable. "Get a job," she declared, a command that cut through the mirage of idyllic escapades. Here's the twist: with a 10th-grade education, an empty wallet, no vehicle to call my own, and a knack for landing on the wrong side of opportunities, finding employment became a puzzle with missing pieces.

To tell the truth, the decision to drop out was a convergence of factors, and if we're being brutally honest, the main trigger was my own laziness, which held a front-row seat in that symphony of choices. I found myself hurtling down the same abyss that generations of my family had descended into. The gravitational pull of that abyss was formidable, but it wasn't just inertia that drove me to that edge.

Absence, they say, makes the heart grow fonder. In my case, the absence of a steadfast male presence in my life led to an abyss of its own. Fatherless, I lacked that compass and guide to steer me through the treacherous terrain of life choices. And as the chorus of indifference grew louder, the voices of responsibility and diligence were drowned out. High school's siren song faded into the background, replaced by the shrill cacophony of apathy. With no role model to instill discipline or echo the importance of education, I succumbed to the gravitational pull of my own disinterest. I walked away without much remorse as if a connection had been severed long before the decision was made. I allowed myself to make the choice to quit school with little regard for the impact it would have on my mother. Frankly, I had reached a point where I just didn't care anymore.

It was a chapter of my life marked by more than just a lack of motivation - it's a tale of a young man lost, navigating the crossroads of ambition and indifference, driven by a mix of rebellion and a pervasive feeling of not giving a damn. A journey where the absence of guidance weighed as heavily as the weight of my own actions.

Yet, as I pen these reflections, it's with a clarity that comes from years of hindsight. While those moments might seem like the stuff of regret, they've paved the way for the person I am today - a person who's wrestled with shadows and emerged stronger. The path I've carved is a testament that even in the darkest chapters, there's the potential for redemption and growth.

In my youth, I never really had a concrete plan for life after high school. The image I held was that of a traditional laborer, making a living by the sweat of my brow and the strength of my back. It was as if my intuition whispered that I was brimming with smarts, yet I was grappling with the riddle of transforming them into something substantial. I was clueless about channeling my intelligence into something beyond basic, manual work.

Dropping out of high school, as uncalculated as it seemed, thrust me into a reality where the immediate need was simple - earning a living. Fortunately, I managed to snag an apprenticeship as a cabinet maker at a company named Andy's Cabinets. I'm eternally thankful for the door that opened for me there. Now, I won't lie; I did my best to sprinkle a bit of trouble-making into the mix, but I excelled in the staining and preparation aspect of the job. Surprisingly, I started raking in some decent money for that period.

Looking back, the choice to part ways with high school holds no regrets for me. In a twist of fate, that decision paved a unique path - one that led me to the army and ultimately to the place I stand today. To this very moment, I hold a conviction that our formal education system falls somewhat short. The question lingers: would the trajectory of my life have been altered for the better had I followed through and obtained that high school diploma? The answer echoes with resolute clarity - a resounding no.

High school, in essence, prepares you for college, a path far from feasible for me. It also imparts some basic hands-on skills, especially in trades like carpentry, which I had the chance to dip into during my 10th grade. So, my 11th and 12th years seemed tailor-made to push me toward college, a notion that was beyond my reach.

As I mentioned earlier, I do believe in the importance of high school for those who set their sights on college. It's the foundation on which the ivory tower is built. However, for those venturing into the trades, its significance diminishes significantly.

\*\*\*

The path less traveled often leaves us with a cocktail of emotions. Leaving high school and diving into the world of cabinet-making did bring a pang of disappointment for missing out on prom. However, in the grand scheme of things, the two years that I devoted to hands-on craftsmanship weren't just about chisels and stains. Those two years I spent working instead of sitting in a classroom played an immeasurable role in steering me toward my path in the army. In essence, those years acted as a turbocharger for my life plan, giving me a chance to earn while I pondered my future. The result was a crystal-clear understanding that a lifetime of manual labor or trade work wasn't where I envisioned myself.

Those two years were my incubation period, a time of introspection and reckoning. They expedited my life's itinerary, allowing me to come to a decision that I might have reached later down the line - unveiling that I didn't want to be confined to labor or the echoes of the workshop forever. My trajectory was set, and while I would eventually have arrived at this juncture after high school, those accelerated years simply allowed me to arrive at the future I envisioned a little sooner.

The crux of the matter, the golden nugget I extracted from that journey, was realizing that those final two years of high school weren't vital for me. I was no stranger to intellect, well-read, and armed with a quick wit. Tackling algebra or another science class wouldn't have contributed much to my personal growth.

When the time eventually came for me to venture into college later on in life, I wasn't weighed down by remedial classes. Instead, I hit the ground running, embracing the learning process with ease. For me, opting out of high school didn't hang heavy with any lasting negative consequences. In retrospect, I realized that high school was a waste of time for me. In fact, it's safe to say that the unconventional path I chose played out well for me.

Wrapping up, let's put a big, bold bow on these life lessons. Here's the grand revelation: early missteps aren't always deal-breakers. Yep, you heard that right. If you make a poor decision early in life, it doesn't always mean it's going to turn out for the worse for you. Just because you had a misadventure or two in your backpack of decisions doesn't mean you're doomed to a life of wrong turns. The beauty lies in the fact that life grants you ample time to pivot and redirect your course.

Think about it - it's like life threw you a curveball, but guess what? You've got the agility to dodge it and swing for the fences. You've got years ahead, a vast terrain to navigate, and plenty of opportunity to swerve, switch lanes, and even make U-turns if you fancy.

But here's where it gets interesting - this double-edged sword swings both ways. This dual nature can be both a challenge and an opportunity. It's a flip of the coin. On one side, it's like having a reset button for your life's path - a chance to leap onto the right track. But here's the kicker: to nail that, you need a secret weapon in the form of strong mentors who have your best interest at heart and can guide you on the right path with insights, nudges, and maybe a well-timed "Hey, maybe don't quit high school just yet."

If I had been blessed with such mentors and a strong father figure who could have nudged me away from quitting high school, my trajectory might have been an earlier college route. But then, I'd have missed out on my army days, my stint as a paratrooper, and all the incredible adventures that followed while I was in the military. So, when I cast a glance backward, I do not dwell on the 'what ifs.' I don't look at it with regret or in a negative light. Instead, it feels like a stroke of fortune, a twist of fate that allowed me to exit high school two years ahead, charting my own course.

Those early choices might not have directly fueled my determination, but they did hand me an experience I wouldn't trade for the world. Funny how the unplanned chapters often become the most cherished ones, right?

# Chapter 5: You're in The Army Now!

For two years, while I worked in the cabinet-making industry, my main gig involved prepping cabinets for their final stages before installation. The cabinets used to be in the last lap before finding their home in custom houses. I'd take in these unfinished pieces, get them all polished up, stain them, and then seal the deal with a lacquer coating. The aim was to shield them from wear and tear.

During this time, I was living at home with my mother and two sisters. The financial landscape was challenging, as my life centered around a modest $3.25 hourly wage. Now, you don't need me to tell you that it's not much to survive on, let alone build a promising future. A bleak realization soon settled in – this job had zero potential for a fruitful future. I realized that sticking to this line of work wouldn't unlock the doors to the future I had in mind. With an old clunker of a car and barely any money to my name, post-high school life looked pretty much the same – not much change in sight.

I held a lifelong aspiration to don the uniform and become a soldier, a dream I painted with romantic colors in my imagination. It seemed like an exciting adventure waiting to unfold. The pivotal moment arrived when I walked into a recruiter's office, diving headfirst into a conversation that would shape my future. The recruiter provided a roadmap of expectations, outlining timelines and the whole deal.

Naturally, the prospect of stepping into the unknown and committing to the army's path was accompanied by a mix of excitement and apprehension. The commitment I was about to make spanned a minimum of four years, which, of course, was a decision not to be taken lightly. My social acumen, apart from what I had gleaned during my high school years, was quite rudimentary. Despite this, I chose to take the plunge to test the waters and see where this unconventional road might lead me. I wouldn't say fear gripped me; instead, a strong sense of purpose guided me, as I believed that this path held more promise than the one I was leaving behind.

Thankfully, I had a brother-in-law who was in the Air Force. His wealth of insights and encouragement injected me with the confidence I needed to believe that I could step into this new chapter (big shout-out to Jack Baker for that!). With his insights and a bolstered sense of fortitude, I embraced the military journey that awaited me, knowing that the challenges ahead were part of the transformational process I had long yearned for.

***

The airplane's hum provided a rhythmic backdrop as the passengers settled into their seats. Amidst the cluster of passengers heading to unknown locations, a boy adorned with long, unkempt hair, $0.00 in his pocket, and attire that spoke of limited resources emerged. This was me, a skinny 18-year-old whose past didn't promise much but whose eyes held a spark of something new.

As the plane soared through the clouds, a girl who was sitting right beside me looked at me and began to make conversation. Her presence was accompanied by an air of warmth and kindness. She was a few years older than me but was very nice. The conversation began like a gentle breeze, tentative at first, then gaining momentum. Her name was Nelda Gonzi. As we exchanged tales, an unspoken camaraderie was forged. Nelda's kindness shone through, and her generosity broke down barriers that distance and circumstance had erected.

Despite my financial emptiness, she generously bought me a couple of drinks on the plane. Nelda was also on her way to join the army as well, and that shared journey formed a bond between us. As we talked, she left a lasting impact on my mind with her simple act of human decency. The sky had surrendered to the inky embrace of the night as the plane touched down in Fort Jackson, South Carolina. The hum of the engine faded, replaced by a hushed anticipation that rippled through the cabin. Neon signs cast a warm glow, guiding the weary travelers as they disembarked onto the tarmac.

A corporal, more of a guardian than a drill instructor, greeted us; he seemed more like a babysitter at the time. His demeanor was friendly, which was an unexpected contrast to the sharp turn fate had in store. As we piled into a van, the bittersweet taste of uncertainty hung in the air. Our path had diverged from the familiar, and we were at the precipice of change. The corporal navigated the streets; this man, though not directly involved in our training, was our guide for the night.

The barracks loomed ahead, and their regimented lines were a testament to the journey that lay ahead. I was in awe of everything around me. The corporal escorted us to a mess hall, granting us a chance to grab a meal before training commenced the following day. The cacophony of voices filled the air as recruits lined up for sustenance, fuel for the battle that awaited them. What really left me amazed was the sight of an all-you-can-eat spread coupled with an endless supply of soda. Now, this is hardly the norm in basic training, where your grub is tightly regulated, though you can eat your fill within those boundaries. Given my past of malnourishment during childhood and adolescence, the unrestricted availability of food and soda was like a dream come true.

As a young man in the midst of this whirlwind experience, the atmosphere and everything unfolding around me felt exhilarating. I had never ventured beyond Tallahassee, which was my home since the age of 11. Fort Jackson was an entirely different universe, unveiling a world of endless possibilities that had been lying in wait.

Fort Jackson brought with it another surprise – its cooler temperature compared to Tallahassee. That cooling breeze put me right at ease. After we were done with the meals, the barracks beckoned, and sleep was a welcome friend after the whirlwind of travel and emotions. In the darkness of the barracks, amidst rows of bunks, camaraderie began to bloom. Conversations wove a tapestry of shared stories, and as the night deepened, the bond between us grew stronger. And in that makeshift family, I started bonding with some of my fellow basic trainees.

That first day at Fort Jackson was not marked by grand events or dramatic encounters, but it carried with it the quiet promise of transformation. And as I drifted into sleep that night, I held within my heart a pocket of gratitude for the kindness of Nelda Gonzi. I often ponder what became of her, and I'd love to reconnect, share this story, and return her kindness in some way. At that time, I was a scrawny 18-year-old with basically nothing to my name, and her simple act of treating me with humanity left a mark that would never fade from my memory.

*\*\**

During the basic training, mentally, I strutted in like a heavyweight champ, a product of my scrappy upbringing. But physically, I seemed more suited for a casual stroll than the rigors of the military. I could barely pump out a measly 10 push-ups, a statistic that felt like an open invitation for the universe to have a good chuckle. Just to twist the knife, the graduation finish line demanded a solid 30 push-ups. My arms were as fond of that idea as a cat is of a bath. This was my biggest weakness.

On the flip side, thankfully, in the physical readiness test triathlon of push-ups, sit-ups, and sprinting, I had some events to boast about. Running like the wind and acing sit-ups were my strong suits, and I owned it. It's funny how life's fairness sometimes balances out your power bars. Yet, the chip on my shoulder remained, along with my penchant for butting heads with authority. This trait, unsurprisingly, landed me in hot water, inviting the drill sergeants' unrelenting focus to knock it out of me.

Amid the haze of basic training, there was that one-time sitcom-worthy moment. Our company's captain ambled over as we were out drilling – a customary rite where the higher-ups haze the recruits. This time was no exception. Amid this scene, a friend of mine became the target of his antics, and I couldn't help but burst into laughter. It struck me as downright comical. Well, my laughter earned me swift retribution. In a flash, Captain Cool zeroed in on me with military-grade precision. I was ordered into push-ups like my life depended on it (which, in basic training, it kinda did). But the pièce de résistance? I was told to stand there while he poured a refreshing canteen shower, administered with icy water all over my head!

Strangely, it didn't bother me. *Did it tick me off?* Not really. *Did it break my laughter spell?* You bet. And while the cold water ran down my spine, so did a newfound realization: maybe keeping my laughter in check around military brass wasn't such a bad idea after all.

***

My first active-duty station after basic training and Advanced Individual Training was the 9<sup>th</sup> Infantry Division, located in Tacoma, Washington. The Army, in its infinite wisdom, decided to post me as far from Tallahassee as possible while keeping me in the US.

The 9th Infantry Division was my inaugural ticket into the whirlwind world of military life. It was more than just another unit - it was the first unit I ever joined and a portal that ushered me into the very heart of what the army was all about. Basic training and advanced individual training were hurdles I'd already leaped over, and now I was at the threshold of my very first assignment. If the army were a story, this was the chapter where it got real.

Having completed basic training and advanced individual training, I was now stationed at my very first assignment. The sun seemed to shine a bit brighter in our neck of the woods, or so it felt. Maybe it was the camaraderie, maybe it was the anticipation of adventures ahead, or maybe it was just a good day to be alive. It was a remarkable setting – excellent weather, a top-notch unit, and standards held high.

Field training exercises were my window into the action-packed life I had chosen. Among those sprawling chow tents, where the aroma of army-cooked spread wide, I received my first initiation into the world of KP - kitchen patrol. Picture this: a vast dining arena, bustling with life as army cooks dished out culinary masterpieces that even a gourmet would applaud.

But fate - or maybe just plain bad luck - decreed that I was the designated clean-up crew. Dishwashing duty, they called it, but it was more like a backstage pass to the army's culinary ballet. Scrubbing dishes might not have sounded glamorous, but amidst the clattering of plates and the rhythm of water, I enjoyed it. It turned out to be quite the experience.

Field deployments were frequent, yet they never truly aligned with a mission. It's important to remember that this was peacetime in the army – we trained hard, honing our skills, but we weren't engaged in active combat.

Then came a pivotal moment in 1984. A plane voyaging from the Middle East to Fort Campbell, the abode of the illustrious 101st Airborne, was tragically downed by terrorists over Gander, Newfoundland. The nation was rocked by this horrifying event. It was during this juncture that I was shuffled from Fort Lewis to Fort Campbell, stepping into the shoes of one of those poor soldiers who died.

Now, I was a part of the 101st Airborne Division! This unit carried a storied legacy, having fought in every major conflict since World War II. It was a symbol of elite status then, as it is today. Here, I flourished, showcasing my leadership prowess and knack for surmounting obstacles to become a formidable soldier. Climbing the ranks, I earned the title of sergeant. I also embarked on numerous deployments and achieved a coveted milestone – my air assault wings. These wings were more than just decorations; they symbolized my proficiency in rappelling out of helicopters and buildings, as well as my ability to sling-load and transport cargo on a helicopter where it was needed. Sporting the "screaming eagle" patch on my left shoulder was exhilarating, to say the least!

Yet, even as I soared to new heights, it was the mentors that supported my growth. A standout was my exceptional platoon sergeant, who saw the potential that simmered within me. He entrusted me with leading a squad, relentlessly encouraging my leadership development.

*** 

The year was 1988 when my long-standing aspiration to join the special forces finally took the driver's seat. The Special Forces had held my fascination like a mesmerizing beacon, and now, the time was ripe to answer that call. So, I steered my course toward Fort Bragg, where a new chapter of my military journey was poised to unfurl.

I began my training, and after completing Morse code school, I dove headfirst into the qualification course. My first parachute jump post-airborne school took me to the historic St. Mere Eglise drop zone – a namesake of the renowned

Normandy location where the 101st Airborne Division made their daring leap on the eve of D-Day.

Navigating special forces school proved demanding, but my physique was on my side – I was slender yet robust and boasted impressive cardiovascular fitness. However, midway through the course, a pivotal life choice loomed ahead. At the age of 22, I had recently tied the knot, and in light of this new chapter, I made the decision to exit the course prematurely. Prioritizing a domestic life alongside my wife became my focus.

Nonetheless, during my service in the Fifth Special Forces Group, I was engaged in numerous missions across the Middle East and Africa. It was during these deployments that I had the privilege of earning my Jordanian jump wings, which are cherished possessions that still hold significant value to me to this day.

Among the countless memories of that time, one stands out as vivid and electrifying as a lightning bolt against the night sky. The scene was set for an airborne infiltration operation - the sort of mission that makes your heart race and your spirit soar. With our gear in place and our readiness tangible, we were a team in sync, moving with a harmony that comes from countless rehearsals and shared experiences. This wasn't our first rodeo; we were seasoned, confident, and ready to embrace the night.

Night jumps always carried an exhilarating edge, cultivating camaraderie and bolstering our self-assurance. The thrill wasn't just in the jump itself but in the unity that it forged and the bonds that tightened during the descent. In those moments, I'd often find myself transported back to an earlier era... to another battlefield. The echoes of history whispered in my ear, and suddenly, I wasn't just a soldier descending from the sky; I was a participant in a grand narrative. In that moment, the vast night sky transformed into the beaches of Normandy, France, on June 5th' 1944! And just like my forefathers' courage and sacrifice coursed through their veins that day, the same infused me with a sense of courage. The echoes of history added an extra layer of significance to my endeavors.

So, on one particular day, we were preparing for a night jump from a C130, a four-turboprop-engine aircraft that served as the Air Force's backbone for heavy lifting. This particular aircraft was one I had jumped from countless times. We weren't just average paratroopers; we were the elite - the special forces, the chosen few who would take to the skies in this mechanical marvel. Our jumps consisted of no more than 16 paratroopers at once. The C130 was our vessel, and that night, it was loaded with our team's aspirations and the promise of a silent and deadly descent.

The scene was set, the stage illuminated by the plane's interior lights. We wore our game faces, yet the camaraderie still bubbled beneath the surface. Jokes were exchanged, spirits high, but as that huge tailgate lowered, a transformation occurred. Laughter turned to focus, and the jovial atmosphere gave way to silence.

The sight from that tailgate was nothing short of awe-inspiring. The C130 banked, and below, Fort Campbell and Clarksville, Tennessee, lit up the night like a shimmering drapery of humanity. Unbeknownst to the people below going about their normal evenings, a battalion of paratroopers was about to quietly paint the sky with their stealthy descent onto the drop zone, only a mile away.

As the commands were given by the jumpmaster, we readied ourselves. When the light turned green and the call of "Go!" resounded, we stepped into the inky void of the night one after another. Leading the team, I was the last to leave the aircraft. I jumped out, and the wind whispered secrets as I fell. I did my four count, and my parachute deployed flawlessly against the backdrop of the moonlit night. It was breathtaking, but luck had other plans. Soon enough, a sense of unease set in as I realized the pilot had released us later than intended, causing the trajectory of two of my men and me to drift toward tall Tennessee pines!

This was the most afraid I had ever been. The looming trees posed a threat, and to compound matters, the quick-release cover on my parachute suspension strap had come loose, revealing the quick-release ring. Talk about a potential recipe for disaster! The separation of the quick-release ring could have led to the loss of my main parachute, leaving me with precious little time to deploy my reserve. Miraculously, this worst-case scenario did not transpire.

Nonetheless, the peril of the trees persisted in my descent. As I plummeted, I braced myself for impact with the pines. Luck was on my side yet again, as I ended up being dragged until I became entangled. Once I felt stable, I deployed my reserve chute and climbed down safely. Thankfully, I emerged unscathed. However, I wasn't alone. My fellow soldiers were in similar arboreal predicaments, entangled in similar trees, so we had to retrieve them later on.

Life within the Fifth Group was a whirlwind of speed, energy, and excitement, maintaining an exceptionally high tempo. Yet, throughout these endeavors, I came to realize that the professionalism displayed by the Green Berets was unmatched. Working alongside these individuals was an experience that truly highlighted their unparalleled dedication and expertise.

*\*\**

Alaska, the land where my military journey reached new heights and the great outdoors became my canvas. My time in Alaska stands out as the pinnacle of my military time. As an outdoors aficionado, I wasn't just in my element; I was thriving in a playground that catered to my every whim. I was a regular in the Alaska wilderness - a moose whisperer, a caribou connector, a rabbit rider, and a bird banterer. If it roamed, flew, or scampered, chances were I had an adventure with it.

However, fishing held the lion's share of my passion, particularly salmon fishing. I was good at it to such an extent that whenever I hit the rivers, my colleagues would jokingly jest that they needed to reel in their lines as I had arrived. Now, whether that's an exaggeration or not, I'll leave it to the legends. What I can confirm is that I caught my limit every time, and my side gig was coaching and helping my fellow anglers reel in their own success stories.

Amidst this backdrop of outdoor pursuits, I embraced new skills. I learned to navigate snow-covered terrains with skiing and snowshoeing. But the significance went beyond leisure. Alaska didn't just teach me about the wild; it also ignited my scholarly side. Inspired by my ever-encouraging wife, I kicked off my college education in this icy wonderland. Who knew that alongside moose and mountains, I'd find the spark for intellectual growth? Moreover, I also became a cold-weather operations and survival expert, adapting to and mastering the challenges presented by frigid climates.

One of the most impactful memories comes to my mind while stationed in Alaska. The place I lived consisted of three townhouses stacked on top of each other, basically a vertical neighborhood. My wife and I inhabited the middle unit, while beneath us resided a Senior NCO, a fellow soldier from my battery whose life was about to collide with ours in a profound way.

It was an ordinary day - or so it seemed. My wife and I had just returned from the gym and were settling into the rhythm of relaxation. Just then, a wild knock shattered the peace. "Loyd, Loyd! Open up. Roxanne has been shot!" The words, laden with panic, were like an electric shock to the system.

I quickly rushed to the door to find that those frantic words were delivered by our neighbor's son, Curtis, who was standing at our doorstep. Following him, his 11-year-old sister, Roxanne, appeared in a state of shock, clutching her left chest. My military training kicked into gear immediately. I assessed her for an exit wound, which she indeed had. Turning to my wife, I said, "Call her mother and tell her I'm rushing her to the hospital!"

Time telescoped into a blur as I raced to my truck while my arms cradled the wounded girl. I positioned her in the passenger seat, and quickly, the tires screeched against the road as I sped to the local hospital. *Everything would be alright!* I thought.

As I carried her into the emergency room, a curious emptiness greeted us; NO ONE WAS THERE. The chaos within me bubbled up, and I shouted, "I have a girl here with a gunshot wound to the chest!"

Instantly, hospital staff emerged from all corners, taking Roxanne from my arms and commencing their efforts. The most challenging moment for me was when they inserted needles into her feet to assess potential paralysis caused by the bullet. Thankfully, the medical team performed admirably. They executed their tasks with precision, ensuring that Roxanne received the care she needed.

Roxanne's ordeal stemmed from an accidental discharge of a .22 caliber rifle in the hands of Curtis during what seemed like harmless play. The bullet found its way into her upper left lung, and once again, luck was on our side – it passed straight through her small frame, leaving a hole where it entered and where it exited.

A thorough inquiry was conducted by my command to understand the incident, and as a result, I was honored with one of my several Army Achievement medals. While this recognition was appreciated, the real victory was Roxanne's survival, marked by a bullet scar and a bad memory.

Alaska was more than just a place; it was the stage where my military journey sparkled like freshly fallen snow. It was a reminder that adventure wasn't just a destination - it was a lifestyle. So, here's to Alaska, where fishing, skiing, academics, and icy exploits converged into a narrative that defined my time in a land as vast and wild as my ambitions.

The next stop in my army uniform was Hawaii - the sun-soaked paradise that served as the backdrop for a chapter of my military journey that unfolded quite differently. In Aloha State, I donned a different kind of uniform: that of a career counselor. It was a role that bore a unique mission - to keep the army ranks filled with the motivated and the committed. As a career counselor, the field wasn't my playground. No muddy boots, no trekking across rugged terrains; my realm was an air-conditioned space - the Triple Army Medical Center. My desk was my command post, and my mission was to ensure that the ones who stood on the edge of reenlistment took the leap into another tour of duty. With a 7:30 AM to 5:00 PM schedule, the stability in this position allowed me to delve into my studies, as I enrolled at Hawaii Pacific University and ultimately earned my bachelor's degree in Business Management.

So, at the end of the day, there's a timeless truth that lingers - a beacon that shines through every twist and turn: the power to better oneself knows no bounds. No matter the hand dealt, there's always room for improvement. The trick lies in peeling back the layers of every situation, like unwrapping the layers of a mystery. Beneath the surface, you'll find the golden truth- there's always a way to level up, even if it's in baby steps. Sculpting your future, one chisel at a time. Think of it as personal evolution.

Moreover, there's a piece of advice I consistently tell everyone: *bet on yourself!* By consistently making the right choices, working diligently, and exercising good judgment, life becomes smoother – not without challenges, but definitely more manageable. Embrace the unknown, confront your fears, and keep forging ahead. And always remember, you're not the first adventurer to tread these paths. Others have wandered before you, conquering mountains of obstacles. You're like a sequel to their story, armed with the knowledge that success leaves breadcrumbs for those who dare to follow.

I often remind myself: *"If he or she can do it, then I can do it too!"* So, when the sun sets, don't just let the curtain fall. Let it rise on a stage where you're the star, and the spotlight is on your journey. Uncover every hidden pathway, uplift yourself with incremental progress, and unleash the potential that's been waiting for its grand debut. You're the protagonist and the hero all rolled into one - you've got this!

# Chapter 6: A Bond Forged in Love

The summer sun hung low in the sky, casting a warm, golden hue over the trailer park where I spent my childhood. I was just eleven years old, an awkward pre-pubescent boy with a mop of unruly hair and a heart that didn't know what it was in for. It was on this very day that I crossed paths with the prettiest woman in my life, Donna.

Donna, a year younger than me at ten, lived a few trailers down. We'd seen each other around the park before, but it was this particular afternoon when our paths finally converged. I was walking by, and as I turned a corner, there she was, like an unexpected oasis in the desert.

Even at that tender age, Donna possessed a beauty that was utterly captivating. Her pretty chestnut hair flowed in the breeze, and her eyes sparkled like a pair of sapphires. My heart skipped a beat, and I felt a strange, unfamiliar sensation stirring within me. Hormones, I would later learn, were beginning to play their unpredictable role.

She was sitting on the front steps of her family's trailer, her bare feet gently swinging back and forth. I hesitated, unsure of what to do or say. Suddenly, she looked at me. As her eyes met mine for the first time, I felt as if time itself had slowed down.

I approached her, and we exchanged names. Our conversation flowed effortlessly from that point on. We discovered that we lived in the same trailer park, and so that was the start of a connection that neither of us could have foreseen.

In the weeks that followed, Donna and I spent countless hours together. We were kind of boyfriend and girlfriend in that innocent, pre-teen way. We shared secrets, laughed at silly jokes, and dreamt of a future that was still a distant mirage. But one memory from those early days stood out vividly.

One sunny afternoon, I visited Donna's mother's office, which was in the city's downtown skyscraper. As we stood in front of the imposing building, our hands brushed against each other. It was as if an electric current surged through my body, and I nervously entwined my fingers with hers.

We stepped into the elevator, and as the doors closed, the world outside faded away. It was just Donna and me, alone in that small, metallic box. My heart raced, and I stole a glance at her. She was blushing, her cheeks a delicate shade of pink. The silence between us was intoxicating, filled with unspoken emotions and the promise of a future we could only imagine.

In that elevator, surrounded by the hum of the city and the beating of our hearts, I knew that this chance encounter was the beginning of a lifelong journey with Donna. Little did I know then that she would become not just the prettiest girl I had ever seen but the love of my life, my confidante, and my partner in all the adventures that lay ahead.

Donna's captivating beauty was just one facet of her charm. What truly drew me to her were her values and personality traits that resonated so strongly with my own. As we grew older, it became clear that Donna and I shared not only a special connection but also a set of deeply held conservative and libertarian values. We were both passionate about individual freedom, limited government, and personal responsibility. Our discussions often revolved around political and philosophical topics, and even though we were still young, our beliefs and convictions were already taking root.

Donna's outgoing nature made her a magnetic presence in our social circles. She effortlessly drew people in with her warm smile and infectious laughter. She had a knack for making everyone feel at ease, and her wit and humor were nothing short of fabulous. Her ability to connect with people was proof of her genuine charm. And in those moments when she shared her conservative and libertarian ideals, she did so with a persuasive eloquence that left even the most ardent skeptics nodding in agreement. Our shared values and her charismatic personality created a bond between us that grew stronger with each passing day.

*\*\**

Returning home from my Army service on leave was always a bittersweet experience. While I cherished the moments spent with my family, there was something else waiting for me, something far more precious than any fleeting vacation: Donna. We had been through so much together, and now, as adults, our relationship had evolved into something more profound.

As my leave progressed, we decided to take our relationship to the next level. It felt like the natural progression of things since that fateful day in the trailer park. We began dating, our connection growing stronger with each passing day. It wasn't long before the idea of marriage started to take root in our hearts.

My family couldn't have been happier for me. They had seen how Donna had grown into a remarkable woman, one who shared my values, my dreams, and my love. To them, she was the perfect match, and their joy was palpable.

However, on the other side of the coin, Donna's family had a different perspective. Her mother and aunt, who had known me since I was a boy, were less than thrilled about our relationship. To them, I was still that same boy, and they struggled to grasp the reality that I had become a man, a soldier no less. Their apprehension about my profession added another layer of complexity to their reservations.

Donna's family was composed of women. They had lived in a matriarchal world, where the concept of a man leading a household was foreign to them. They couldn't easily fathom the idea of submission to a man or allowing a man to take the lead in their lives. As someone who had grown into a strong leader myself, I couldn't help but balk at this.

In our journey towards marriage, there were moments of tension and misunderstanding. The clash of our worlds, where tradition met modernity, created friction that was hard to ignore. However, as time passed, they began to accept that I was now the leader in Donna's life. It was a change that happened not out of choice but out of necessity, as our love was too strong to be denied.

\*\*\*

The sun was beginning to set over Cumberland County, casting a soothing, golden shimmer over the courthouse where Donna and I were about to exchange our vows. The historic building stood in the shadow of Fort Bragg, a place that had been a significant part of my life as an Army soldier. It seemed only fitting that we'd choose this courthouse for our wedding day.

Inside, the courthouse buzzed with activity, but our attention was fixed on the momentous occasion ahead. Donna, radiant in her simple yet elegant dress, held my arm with a nervous yet excited smile. My heart swelled with love and anticipation as we awaited our turn before the judge.

The judge presiding over our wedding ceremony was a kindly African-American woman with a warm smile. She held a stack of papers in her hands, her voice steady as she began to officiate the union of two childhood friends turned lovers. Yet, there was a humorous twist to this solemn moment.

As the judge spoke, she repeatedly stumbled over Donna's name, turning it into "Donner." Each time she mispronounced it, Donna would give me a sideways glance, her eyes dancing with suppressed laughter. And then, when it was my turn, the judge called me "Lord" instead of "Loyd." We couldn't help but chuckle at her friendly but persistent blunders, the tension in the room giving way to shared mirth.

The guests in the courtroom joined in our laughter, and it was in that moment, amidst the lightness and joy, that we exchanged our vows. After exchanging our vows and rings, we sealed our commitment with a kiss, surrounded by the echoes of our own amusement and the endearing imperfections of our wedding ceremony.

Later that evening, we celebrated at a cozy restaurant named 'Chichi's' with two of my friends from Special Forces school. As we savored our meals and shared stories, we couldn't help but overhear a conversation from an adjacent table - a black couple making a rather bold comment. "I don't give it six months," one of them remarked.

Donna and I exchanged amused glances. Little did they know that we had already been through so much together, and our love was as strong as the bonds of time. We kept our composure, but the humor in their remark lingered with us, becoming a memory that we still laugh about to this day.

Our wedding day was not grand or extravagant, but it was filled with love, laughter, and the promise of a lifetime together - a day that marked the beginning of a journey that continues to this very moment, a journey built on love, shared dreams, and the enduring strength of our bond.

One of the unique aspects of our early marriage was the distance from our respective families. While it may seem challenging, it turned out to be a blessing. It allowed Donna and me to learn to be husband and wife on our terms, without the influence or interference of meddling family members. We navigated the challenges, celebrated the successes, and built a life together, forging a bond that was uniquely our own.

As with any marriage, our journey was not without its ups and downs, the highs and lows that are an inevitable part of any long-lasting relationship. In our earlier years, we faced our fair share of challenges. Like many young couples, we brought our own individual egos and expectations into the marriage. This sometimes led to conflicts and misunderstandings as we navigated the delicate balance of power and decision-making in our relationship.

Donna, strong-willed and independent, had her own vision of how things should be, as did I. We both had our moments of asserting our opinions and desires, sometimes clashing in the process. It was a period of adjustment, where we had to find our way through the maze of emotions and desires that often accompany the early stages of marriage.

But over time, our marriage evolved, and we both grew. Donna became more understanding of her role as my partner, and I, in turn, learned to appreciate her wisdom and perspective. It was a journey of mutual growth and understanding.

It's been 35 years, and I can say for sure that marriage has a unique way of shaping and refining us. In my case, it was Donna who played a significant role in civilizing and polishing me over the years. I had been a wildcat, untamed and unbridled, but through the years with Donna, I had transformed into a semi-feral cat, still wild at heart but with a touch of refinement. I used to have my own set of rough edges and untamed qualities. But Donna, with her patience, grace, and firm love, got on board the journey of guiding me toward becoming a more refined version of myself.

With her innate sense of style and substance, she gave me advice on how to present myself to the world. She helped me understand the importance of dressing well and taking pride in my appearance. I'll admit that, at times, I might have been resistant to change, clinging to my old ways, but Donna's gentle encouragement and belief in my potential gradually won me over. Her advice became a source of personal growth, and I came to appreciate the positive impact it had on my life.

Today, I look back on our journey with gratitude for the woman who not only became my wife but also my guide and mentor in the art of living a well-rounded and fulfilling life. Our love has endured and deepened, and as we look back on our 35-year journey together, we do so with gratitude for the laughter, the love, and the lessons learned along the way, knowing that the best is yet to come.

***

When a guy marries, he automatically thinks about having children. I, being a human, had aspirations to be a dad too. However, I had no idea how and what it would all come down to.

It all began during a vacation my wife took to Alaska to visit her family, a trip that would lead to a chance encounter that would shape our future. During her visit, my wife met her nine-month-old niece, Laura. This little bundle of joy was full of life, running around and innocently declaring the presence of her 'imaginary daddy' named Jeffrey. Laura's innocence and her yearning for stability touched our hearts deeply. It was in that moment that my wife felt a strong desire to ensure that Laura had the stable family life she deserved, a life with both a father and a mother who could provide her with love and security.

We never really went through the formal process of adoption for Laura and Zach; we took full, long-term custody of them. Our hope was that by providing them with the stability of a loving family, we could positively influence their journey from childhood to adulthood. We had to make a decision, but if I am honest, I must admit that I'm a rather impulsive person by nature. There wasn't a particular moment of deep reflection or a grand epiphany; we simply made the decision and ran with it. It felt like the right thing to do, and we trusted our instincts. It was a choice born out of love and a deep sense of responsibility.

However, it wasn't all smooth sailing. We had to face my sister-in-law's aunt, Beth, who had developed a strong attachment to the children, considering them as her own. Beth, a single woman with no children of her own and no husband, was reluctant to give them up. It became clear that we would need to take legal action to secure their custody.

To formalize our custody arrangement, we had to take both Beth and the birth mother to court. Our goal was to outline a recovery plan for the birth mother to change her life track in order to regain custody. While we understood the desire for family reunification, deep down, we realized that it was unlikely she would take the necessary steps, and that realization ultimately worked in our favor in the long run. As time passed, it became increasingly apparent that Laura and Zach's best interests were served by being with us in a loving and stable home.

Now that Laura and Zach had come into our house, the dynamics had changed. Becoming a parent at 22 was a daunting experience, one that brought a whirlwind of change into my life. I had spent my early adulthood in the Army, learning a set of skills and values that, while invaluable in their own right, were not necessarily geared toward parenting. Yet, there I was, a young man with a four-year-old daughter, suddenly responsible for guiding another life.

Parenthood, I quickly realized, was an entirely different battlefield, and I was thrust into it with little training or preparation. The military way of doing things, while effective in its own context, often proved less than optimal when dealing with the nuances of raising children. I found myself navigating uncharted waters, relying on instinct, and learning as I went along.

As my wife and I embraced our roles as parents to Laura and Zach, we soon discovered that the age-old adage 'nature over nurture' held true in many aspects of their lives. Both of them displayed characteristics inherited from their birth mother, traits that often included a lack of concern for anything but themselves, a touch of narcissism, and a tendency towards selfishness. These traits presented challenges, especially when it came to motivation and academic performance. School was a particularly difficult area for both of them.

In contrast, our biological son seemed to possess the opposite set of traits. He excelled in various aspects of his life, demonstrating motivation, empathy, and a genuine interest in learning and growth. It was a stark reminder that while nurture played a significant role in a child's development, nature had its own undeniable influence.

Despite these challenges, we never gave up on Laura and Zach. We believed in their potential and saw glimpses of the people they could become. It was a journey that tested our limits and demanded a deep reservoir of love and understanding.

As time passed, our journey as parents continued to evolve, with each child following a unique path in life. We witnessed the incredible resilience of human nature, particularly in our eldest, Laura. She managed to turn her life around, defying the odds stacked against her. She blossomed into a remarkable young woman and joined the Air Force, a decision that would provide her with structure and purpose. She became a mother herself and, against all expectations, flourished in her new role. Today, she is a source of pride and inspiration, proof of the power of fortitude and the transformative potential within us all. I and Donna couldn't be more proud of her.

We are not only proud of her accomplishments but also deeply grateful for the strong bond we share. Laura had transformed her life, and she was now raising her own 16-year-old son with love, care, and dedication. Our relationship with her is a source of joy and fulfillment, a testament to the enduring power of family.

However, the road with our middle son, Zach, was much more challenging and heart-wrenching. He fell into the grip of addiction, a battle that is one of the most agonizing experiences for any parent to witness. Despite our best efforts, his journey had taken a dark turn, leading us to a point where we now have no contact with him whatsoever.

*** 

Marriage, for me, was a transformative experience, one that brought both growth and a deeper sense of responsibility. It had a civilizing effect, molding me into a more refined version of myself. Through the institution of marriage, I learned to focus on more than just my own needs and desires. The arrival of children amplified that sense of responsibility, reminding me that life was no longer solely about me but about nurturing and caring for a growing family.

As I look back, I think that oftentimes, we get on board our life's path with the best intentions, believing that the choices we make are the right ones for our family and friends. We carry a sense of duty and a deep commitment to those we love, and we believe that our actions will be met with appreciation and gratitude.

However, the reality of life is complex, and sometimes, our best intentions can lead to unanticipated challenges and outcomes. The journey of adoption or taking on the care of family members can be filled with moments of great love and joy, but it can also be fraught with difficulties. I would seriously caution anyone who is thinking about adopting or trying to take care of any family member's child because, at the end of the day, it's a path that may, at times, be marked by unappreciation and ingratitude, both from the children we care for and the biological family members involved.

I am speaking from my own experience, which is a reminder that such journeys can be incredibly demanding, emotionally and mentally, and it's essential to approach them with a clear understanding of the potential challenges that may arise. In the face of these challenges, it's key to maintain one's sense of self and boundaries to ensure that your own well-being and happiness are not sacrificed in the process. Parenthood and caregiving are acts of deep love, but they also require self-care and the preservation of your own happiness and peace of mind.

In the end, the journey of love, marriage, and parenthood is a deeply personal and unique one, with its own set of joys and trials. It's an expedition that evolves over time, teaching us valuable lessons about ourselves, our capacity for love, and the complexities of human relationships. And through it all, it is the lasting power of love that sustains us, helping us navigate the intricate pattern of family life with all its trials and rewards.

# Gallery

*Young me in my favorite suit*

*Yes, that's me as a kid.*

*Me and my canine companion, Lady.*

*In my proud 5th Group uniform*

*Standing tall in uniform, ready for the Jordon Jump.*

*In the untamed Alaskan wilderness, I stand before a majestic caribou, holding its proud antlers.*

*Holding a big fish, with innocent little Laura by my side.*

*I stand rugged and gritty in the Alaskan snow, holding an M16.*

*Clad in military garb, showcasing the medals on my chest.*

*Surrounded by the timeless beauty of Uluru, embracing the magic of the Australian landscape.*

*A visual representation of my body transformation*

*Celebrating my victory in Brazilian Jiu-Jitsu*

*Presenting my hard-earned medals, highlighting my journey in Brazilian Jiu-Jitsu.*

# Chapter 7: Beyond the Uniform

Joining the military is more like getting a turbo boost in the game of life. I sometimes feel military life is the ultimate crash course in discipline, honor, and the art of getting things done, even if you have to move mountains. Plus, for those of us not born with silver spoons in our mouths, it's a reliable paycheck that comes with a side of fantastic friendships and top-notch training. So, it's a life upgrade package with a dash of camaraderie thrown in for good measure!

My journey in the military was a true game-changer in my life. When I enlisted, I was pretty much broke, with little prospect of making money. Joining the army was my ticket out of the poverty trap, and it turned out to be an incredibly positive experience. I encountered my fair share of challenges and successes, but I'd say the latter definitely outweighed the former.

The Army had a quirky sense of humor, deciding to send a country boy from Florida all the way across the country to Fort Lewis, Washington, for my first duty station. It was a journey that took me from the swamps to the mountains, and boy, did it open up a world of experiences I could never have anticipated.

Arriving at Fort Lewis in the heart of winter, January 1985, was like stepping into a snow-covered wonderland. While I'd encountered snow before, this was a whole new level. The landscape was transformed, with spruces and firs blanketed in white, creating a picturesque scene that filled me with delight.

My time at Fort Lewis began in a rather unremarkable manner as I served as a motor pool clerk for about a year. However, 1986 brought a turning point when tragedy struck. A plane returning from the Middle East was tragically blown up by terrorists in Gander, Newfoundland. Among the victims were over 200 soldiers from the esteemed 101st Airborne Division. As I mentioned earlier, I found myself slated to replace one of those fallen heroes. It marked my first encounter with an elite unit.

The 101st Airborne Division boasted a storied history, having fought valiantly in World War II and Vietnam. Wearing the iconic 'Screaming Eagle' on my uniform filled me with an overwhelming sense of pride and purpose. My transfer to Fort Campbell marked a significant turning point in my military career. It was there that I realized that with dedication and stanch effort, I could truly excel as a soldier.

My journey continued as I decided to take on new challenges and opportunities within the military. One of the first stops on this path was attending Air Assault School, often touted as one of the toughest ten days in the Army. To my surprise, it didn't prove as formidable as its reputation. The school was divided into three phases, and I found myself excelling in each one. Graduating from this demanding course allowed me to proudly wear the coveted Air Assault wings on my uniform.

Leaving Fort Campbell, I set my sights on an even more challenging endeavor: joining the Special Forces. My next stop was Airborne School at Fort Benning, Georgia, where I successfully earned the prestigious airborne wings that I mentioned earlier. To this day, I hold that achievement in high regard.

My journey took me to Fort Bragg, North Carolina, where I got aboard the rigorous Special Forces training program, marking the next chapter in my military career. However, midway through my training, I had an "aha" moment and decided to shift my focus towards my marriage, being a freshly minted newlywed and all. The Army then decided to spice things up by sending me to Fairbanks, Alaska, which felt like they'd tossed me into a deep-freeze adventure with the 6th Infantry Division. There, I became a maestro in military operations amidst the frosty Arctic surroundings and earned my stripes as a cold weather survival specialist. And I didn't stop there – I even attended rappel master school, which allowed me to conduct air assault operations.

After my icy Alaskan escapade, I made my way back to the welcoming embrace of Fort Campbell and rekindled my love affair with the Special Forces. While part of the illustrious Fifth Group, I had the privilege of attending one of the military's most sought-after schools: the Survival Evasion Resistance and Escape School, or as it's commonly known, SERE School.

The Survival Evasion Resistance and Escape School was a place I forged fond memories, but let's be honest, it pretty much sucked the entire time. It was a crash course in everything from surviving in the wild with the bare minimum to artfully dodging enemy forces and even mastering the fine art of resisting interrogation and those pesky attempts to convert a soldier. But perhaps the best part was the escape and reunion mission – a real-life game of cat and mouse.

Despite the hardships, it was hands down my favorite school experience and probably the most valuable one, too. After conquering SERE, I decided to switch gears and transitioned into the role of a career counselor. It was here that I had the opportunity to guide and educate fellow soldiers on the path to retaining their place in the army.

My journey continued, taking me to Fort Carson, Colorado, where I welcomed the birth of my son. And then, the cherry on top, I found myself at Tripler Army Medical Center in sunny Honolulu, Hawaii. What a whirlwind adventure it has been!

The military was my ticket to growing up, no doubt about it. Before enlisting, I was just a scrawny, know-it-all redneck with a bit of a thug attitude. I thought I had life all figured out, and my cocky arrogance knew no bounds. But the military had other plans for me. It taught me the art of mission accomplishment, no matter the cost. In the military, the mission always takes top billing, and everything else is relegated to the backseat. This valuable lesson also taught me about honor, discipline, and the power of perseverance.

You see, the army is a constant battle of challenges. Every field exercise, deployment, or school demands peak performance, or you'll quickly find yourself replaced. This crucible of high expectations showed me that I could rise to the occasion and meet any requirement thrown my way.

I would say the military didn't just mold me; it gave me a sense of identity. It set me apart from my friends back home, creating a unique bond that only veterans truly understand. To this day, I cherish my military service, fully aware that most people will never sign up for the rollercoaster ride I embarked upon. And even among fellow veterans, my experience stands as proof of the exceptional accomplishments and experiences that came my way.

***

Upon entering the military, one of the first things that struck me was the realization that, deep down, I was just as intellectually capable as most of the officers higher up the chain of command. There was, however, one glaring difference: they had college degrees. So, as I neared the completion of my own degree, I faced a crossroads.

Balancing the responsibilities of raising three children with a wife while serving as a Staff Sergeant was a challenging endeavor. It dawned on me that trying to make a living, raise three kids, and keep a wife happy on a staff sergeant's salary was a recipe for anything but success. Despite 15 years of dedicated service, my base pay was a modest $25,000 per year. With a family to support, it became evident that this income wasn't sustainable.

At this juncture, I had also earned my bachelor's degree and recognized that the civilian sector offered more lucrative opportunities. After a decade and a half of faithful service, I made the tough decision to hang up my military boots and bid farewell to the Army, with the goal of pursuing my master's degree and forging a career in the civilian world.

Leaving the military was an exhilarating prospect for me. I was eager to dive headfirst into the world of graduate school, contemplating the paths of law school or pursuing my MBA. But what truly tickled my fancy was the thought of shedding the military's strict regimen. Don't get me wrong; I had no intention of turning into a couch potato. It just meant I was no longer tangled in the web of those tiresome military rules that cling to soldiers like shadows.

In those 15 years of service, I collected more knowledge than a library card on steroids. And guess what? I'm still cashing in on that wisdom today. It's like having a treasure chest of life lessons at my fingertips, and I couldn't be more grateful for the journey that led me here.

\*\*\*

Leaving the military was a breeze, except for one tiny detail: I was still carrying around that military mindset. What it boiled down to was that I had a work ethic and outlook that set me apart from the civilian crowd, and truth be told, it still does today. Dealing with the laissez-faire attitudes of most civilians was like trying to fit a square peg into a round hole – a bit of a head-scratcher, to say the least. Many civilians seemed to lack the same level of dedication, physical prowess, industriousness, and mission-oriented mindset that I had honed during my military service. It was apparent that I operated on a different frequency.

In fact, rather than struggling to adapt, I found that my military background gave me a distinct advantage. It propelled me to excel amidst this civilian landscape, where I stood out like a shining star. The discipline, work ethic, and focus I had cultivated in the military turned out to be my secret weapons for thriving in the civilian world. But yes, over time, I've managed to soften my approach and become a bit more of a gentle communicator.

As I look back now, I realize there wasn't much of a support system waiting for me on the outside, aside from my steadfast family and my ever-patient wife. They were the sturdy pillars that helped me weather the adjustment storm. Not to forget that when you leave the military, you also bid adieu to its robust support structure, including perks like housing benefits, auto shops, woodshops, commissaries, and the post exchange – all those conveniences you once took for granted. It's a clean break, a sudden plunge into independence. Moreover, you're distanced from the comrades and friends you formed deep bonds with during your military journey.

Nevertheless, I've always had a strong belief in myself and in my incredible wife's ability to navigate this new chapter. I knew we could ensure the well-being of our family, so I didn't dwell on what was left behind.

As for my career path, I was confused and torn between pursuing a legal education or going for a graduate degree in business. I decided to dig deep and do some research. What I unearthed was quite enlightening: the long-term financial prospects for MBAs outshone those for lawyers. Plus, the business school I had my sights on offered an accelerated program, meaning I'd be out in the workforce making money within a year. It felt like a smart move, and I was ready to dive into this new adventure.

During my Graduate School days, I clung to my routines like a lifeline. The daily workouts - those three to five miles of pavement-pounding every other day – were non-negotiable. Call it dedication or perhaps a touch of stubbornness, but I was determined to stay in top-notch shape while pursuing my academic endeavors.

And Excel I did! Graduate School became my intellectual playground, where I thrived academically and consistently raised the bar for myself. But here's the twist: beneath the surface of academic achievements, I grappled with a curious conundrum. My identity seemed largely tethered to my military past, leaving me with a distinct lack of other self-defined facets. It was as if my military service had cast a long shadow, one that still influences how I perceive myself today and maybe, just maybe, adds a certain militaristic flair to my everyday life.

The paramount lesson I gleaned from bidding farewell to the military after 15 years is a nugget of wisdom I wholeheartedly share with those facing layoffs, terminations, or the daunting prospect of change in their lives. That lesson is simple yet profound: ***bet on yourself.***

When the safety net of the familiar falls away, when the uniform is hung up for good, and the future seems uncertain, it's essential to recognize the incredible potential and resilience that resides within you. Trust in your abilities, your adaptability, and your capacity to carve a new path. Betting on yourself is not a gamble; it's a surefire investment in your own capabilities and the limitless possibilities that await your courageous step forward.

Like it or not, we all have to accept a fundamental truth: change can be intimidating, but it's seldom a life-or-death proposition. In fact, more often than not, change brings about positive outcomes – though we might not recognize them until further down the road.

Furthermore, consider putting yourself in a position where you can confidently bet on yourself. When the chips are down and the world feels uncertain, your belief in your abilities becomes your most valuable asset. Ultimately, it's all you truly have.

Lastly, let me leave you with this piece of advice: aim to do a little better each and every day. You might not be where I am today, or perhaps you're already farther along the path, but one thing is certain – you will be better than you were yesterday. So, stay committed to your journey, keep grinding, and keep pushing forward because progress, no matter how incremental, is the key to reaching your goals.

# Chapter 8: Unveiling New Horizons

*As the sun sets on the familiar landscapes of our past,*
*We stand on the threshold of a new dawn, steadfast.*
*The world before us is a picture of uncharted skies, Unveiling new*
*horizons where our dreams will rise.*

*With each step forward, we embrace the unknown,*
*In search of wisdom, adventures to be sown.*
*New horizons signal promising grand surprise,*
*As we unlock the secrets hidden in the world's endless ties.*

*The journey ahead is filled with wonder and grace, Challenges to conquer*
*in this boundless space.*
*We'll chart our course through uncharted seas,*
*Unveiling new horizons, with hearts full of ease.*

Life is full of wonders and opportunities. If you step out and into the unknown and get scared, it can feel like the end of the road. But if you take a moment to relax, breathe, and look closely, you'll find numerous opportunities waiting for you to seize. Of course, it takes work and determination to explore these new possibilities, but it's not impossible.

My own story is a lot like this. My main reason for pursuing higher education was to provide for my family in a way I never had before. Additionally, I've always been a lifelong learner, an ardent reader, and an unceasingly curious soul. This quest for knowledge and the courage to explore the unknown has opened doors I never imagined, proving that with tenacity and vision, you can truly unlock the boundless potential that life has to offer.

These flames of my curiosity have burned brightly from the very start. As time passed, my literary preferences have steered clear of the fictional. Instead, I prefer to read and explore the world of business tomes, gripping biographies, and the storied pages of history. It's my deliberate choice, motivated by a thirst for knowledge, that continues to propel me forward.

Donna and I have always shared an open and candid dialogue about our wants and needs. I distinctly recall having a conversation with her regarding my decision to pursue further education, and she was exceptionally supportive throughout the entire process.

When I decided to embark on my journey to graduate school, my children were quite young. Their world revolved around basic needs: food, shelter, and clothing, which we were steadfast in providing. Of course, my wife played a crucial role in facilitating this support. While I pursued my graduate studies, she assumed the role of the primary breadwinner, working tirelessly to ensure that we had everything we required during this period. Without her firm devotion and hard work, I have serious doubts about whether I would have successfully completed my education.

I must admit there were moments of self-doubt and insecurity. After all, this was an entirely new chapter in my life, and I was a mere 34 years old. It was a venture into an unfamiliar ground, and I didn't have the luxury of experience to lean on. Nevertheless, deep down, I carried a robust sense of self-confidence. The military's "mission first" outlook had instilled in me a strong belief that failure was not an option. My family was counting on me, and that commitment bolstered my fortitude.

Surprisingly, when it came to building confidence for my academic pursuits, I didn't encounter weighty challenges. Failure simply wasn't in my vocabulary; it never even grazed my thoughts. My mindset was resolute, steadfast in its chase of knowledge, and utterly gritty to succeed.

While boarding on the journey to Graduate School, the looming specter of rejection was the sole uncertainty that niggled at my thoughts. Yet, I brought some formidable credentials to the table, boasting a sturdy 3.75 GPA from my undergrad days. What further strengthened my confidence were the personal statements penned by my professors, who kindly vouched for my abilities and character, helping me make a favorable impression.

So, you can imagine the sheer thrill that coursed through me when that long-anticipated acceptance letter from FSU arrived in my mailbox. It was an electrifying moment. Attending my hometown school had always been a cherished dream, and to see it materialize was an incredibly exciting and gratifying turn of events.

\*\*\*

The moment I set foot on the historic campus of Florida State University, founded way back in 1851, I couldn't help but admire the timeless beauty that surrounded me. The university exuded an old-world charm, with antebellum architecture that lent an air of timeless beauty to the surroundings. It would be an understatement to say that the architecture was indeed really beautiful and maybe the perfect place to begin my academic journey.

However, I'd be remiss if I didn't admit to a flicker of doubt on that very first day. As a military veteran, I wondered how my education stacked up against the younger civilian students bustling around me. They seemed full of youthful enthusiasm and fresh perspectives. It was natural to question if I could hold my own in this new academic environment. But, as the days went by, my concerns began to dissipate. By the end of that first day, I discovered that not only could I keep pace, but I often outshone many of my classmates. My military experience had imparted a strong work ethic and a unique perspective that set me apart.

Among the plethora of subjects I studied during my graduate, entrepreneurship was one of my most captivating and enduring fascinations. There's something electric about the art of conceiving, shaping, and building businesses from the ground up. It's a world where innovation, risk, and creativity meld into a dynamic force that ignites my passion. Looking into the details of business shaping and deal-making was equally enthralling. The art of negotiation, making agreements, and steering the course of a business's growth rang to me on a different level. These are skills that remain close to my heart even to this day.

One of the significant moments in my graduate pursuit was when I had a conflict with one of my professors, Dr. Osteryoung. It was clear to me that this individual had a personal issue with me, which I assumed might be due to our stark differences. I stood tall at 6'3", exuding a certain confidence and swagger that didn't sit well with everyone. To put it mildly, not everyone appreciated my demeanor. Dr. Osteryoung, on the other hand, was, well, quite the opposite –

short, stocky, and, to be frank, not the most pleasant person to be around.

But let me be clear: this professor, Dr. Osteryoung, was not just someone I had a minor disagreement with. He was a total jerk. Our mutual animosity was undeniable; he didn't like me, and I certainly didn't like him in return. Even with my confidence and swagger, it was from him that I gathered one of the most significant lessons during my time in college. It was not one of wisdom but rather an example of what not to be, i.e., a piece of shit. This guy treated me unfairly, and I couldn't help but wonder how he even ended up in a position to shape young minds. I'll always remember him as a total... well, let's just say he was far from a pleasant individual.

But hindsight has a way of coloring things in an interesting light. Looking back, there's an overwhelming sense of contentment in realizing that I now earn over three times as much as him. The old saying, "Those who can do, and those who can't teach," seems to ring truer than ever. This realization has solidified itself over the course of my two-decade-long career in the business world.

It's not to say that those with PhDs aren't incredibly knowledgeable in their fields; they certainly are, but their expertise is largely rooted in academic theory. Real-world application is an entirely different beast. When it comes to applying these theories and techniques, we often find that they must be adapted and fine-tuned to accommodate various factors. Chief among these is the human element, and a close second is the lightning-paced evolution of the business landscape.

In business, change is the only constant. Adaptation, practicality, and the ability to navigate the interplay of human factors are what truly set apart those who thrive in the business world. As time has taught me, the academic arena may serve as a solid foundation, but it's out there in the field where theories meet reality and where the true lessons are learned.

Donna and I often reflect on the fact that pursuing my MBA was one of the best decisions we ever made. It opened doors that I hadn't even known existed. My first job after completing grad school with Accenture did more than just boost my income; it sent it skyrocketing. In fact, my earnings more than doubled my basic army pay.

But the perks didn't stop at the paycheck. My MBA, in a way, turned out to be our passport to incredible adventures and experiences we once thought were beyond our reach. We've traveled to places we'd only dreamed of, exploring a world we couldn't have imagined during my military service. All in all, it's safe to say that this educational pursuit has truly been a life-changing game-changer for us.

As a concluding thought, if you're considering college or a graduate degree, make sure you're doing it for yourself, with a clear purpose in mind. Don't succumb to external pressures, whether from well-intentioned parents or the appeal of wealth, because education is about much more than that.

Have the courage to challenge yourself to venture outside your comfort zone. It's in these moments of self-imposed challenge and discovery that you'll unearth your true potential. It all starts with the mindset of daring to venture beyond the familiar. Self-doubt may creep in, but remember that you possess the same caliber of talent, intelligence, and skills as anyone else. Your potential knows no bounds when you believe in yourself and your abilities. So, go ahead, take those leaps, break through those barriers, and watch how your personality blooms.

Lastly, remember this: if it has been done before, then you can do it too. Embrace your ambitions, set your goals, and pursue them with solid purpose. The road may be grueling at times, but the journey is rich with the rewards of self-discovery and personal growth. Your degree is just the prologue to your adventure; the rest of the story is penned by your passion and perseverance. So, go forth, conquer your doubts, and script a tale worth telling!

# Chapter 9: Ego is the Enemy

Growing up poor, I had my fair share of encounters with bullies. Early on, I learned the importance of standing up for myself and doing so resolutely. This experience instilled in me a fighting spirit that would serve me well in the years to come.

One curious facet of my personality that's been a constant companion is the proverbial "chip on my shoulder." I was never the poster child for physical prowess – not the most handsome, not the strongest, not the fastest, and certainly not the biggest. This led to a concoction of insecurity sprinkled with a generous dash of bravado. It's a peculiar mix, really – feeling vulnerable while simultaneously exuding an air of unshakable self-confidence.

I always knew that my intelligence was my strong suit and a mouth that could slice through steel. I have a vivid memory of beating one of my stepfathers in a game of chess when I was a mere 11 years old. The poor man was in his mid-30s, and I must admit, he didn't quite handle the fact that a pre-teen was consistently outsmarting him. Victory was always within my grasp, and he never once tasted it. I recall him flipping the chessboard in frustration on numerous occasions. Even at the age of 11, I relished rubbing my victories in his face, and I did so with unapologetic confidence.

My ego, I must admit, has had its moments in the spotlight, both for better and for worse. While it's certainly put me in some tricky situations, it's also been a driving force behind my personal growth and resilience. There's a vivid memory of a time when I decided to channel my inner snark in a series of emails. I went for the direct and no-nonsense approach, but it ended up causing quite the kerfuffle between myself, my colleagues, and the upper echelons of management. I couldn't escape the repercussions of my audacious behavior, and I had to answer for my indiscretions.

It's safe to say that in my youth, my self-confidence often got tangled up with an unwarranted sense of ego. The ego, though, didn't truly earn its stripes until later in life. It's a peculiar thing because, on the one hand, it's driven me forward, but on the other, it's tripped me up on numerous occasions.

There's been a recurring theme in my life – a reluctance to back down from a fight, an inclination to take every challenge as a personal affront. This has certainly left a mark on my relationships, both in the business world and in personal connections. Only in recent years have I come to the realization that to truly thrive and succeed, one must learn to keep one's ego in check.

The skirmishes with my wife, my friends, and my colleagues have been far from beneficial. It was a constant clash of egos, mine and theirs, creating a perfect storm of discord. If I could turn back time and share some wisdom with my younger self, and I now pass this wisdom on to my son, it would be this: Ego is the enemy. It's the chief culprit behind most conflicts among men. Yet, it's also a force that can be tamed and easily managed with the right approach.

The clashes fueled by ego didn't necessarily leave me with devastating consequences, but they did prove to be a considerable hindrance when it came to forming meaningful relationships. It wasn't about wounded pride or bruised feelings; it was the fiery anger that ignited when someone dared to challenge me. I never possessed the patience to pause and reflect, choosing instead to react swiftly and often with an intensity that was more akin to a volcanic eruption.

Recalling the episode with the high school football player I mentioned earlier is a prime example, but it's far from an isolated incident in my life's narrative. These eruptions of ego-driven conflict have punctuated my journey, leaving me to ponder the potential connections and opportunities that may have been missed due to my eagerness to assert myself rather than engage in constructive dialogue.

There have been a couple of instances when my penchant for confrontation reared its head. One such incident took place during my time in the army. A fellow soldier brought a woman and her young son to the barracks. A friend of mine and I were in there playing ping pong when the little kid was left unattended in the day room, and I felt it was a safety concern as he kept closing the door to the pool room. So, I repeatedly asked him to leave the door open for safety's sake.

However, he immediately reported my request to his mother, and the soldier, Ezel Trouble, confronted me. I explained that I was only looking out for the child's well-being, but he was in no mood for reason and kept running his mouth. He kept provoking the situation, so, of course, I challenged him to step outside for a mano-a-mano resolution. Our dispute turned into a fistfight, with me emerging as the victor, though he did manage to bite me in the process. Looking back, I could've tried to de-escalate the situation, but Ezel's provocations led me down a different path, one where I believed he needed to learn a lesson.

Then, there was that more recent incident in Puerto Rico. My friends and I had rented surfboards, but I was struggling to catch a wave, so I decided to return the boards the next day. When I asked the proprietor for a refund, he bluntly declined. My threat to involve my credit card company was like tossing gasoline onto an open flame of his ego. He flew into a fit of rage, yelling and making threats. Naturally, I didn't take this kindly, and my own ego fired back, calling him every name in the book and reducing him to feeling like a big pushover. Looking back, it's clear that a calmer approach would have been the wiser choice, and I could have handled that better.

When I reflect on my experiences, both in the military and in the civilian world, it's quite evident that my ego has had a notable impact. In my military career, it often served me well because it's an environment where directness, determination, and a strong presence are valued traits. Establishing yourself as a competent leader, a resilient soldier, and a devoted professional is the name of the game. On the flip side, in the civilian world, these same qualities can occasionally hinder your path to success. In this realm, things get a bit more complex, and the terrain is often shaped by the intricacies of politics.

I have learned the hard way that it's generally better to build relationships than to damage them. Prioritizing relationship-building is paramount, as it never carries a downside. It's a concept I like to emphasize – you can either strengthen a relationship, maintain it at a neutral level, or erode it. Nurturing strong relations makes the other person feel respected, valued, and appreciated. Consequently, when you require assistance or cooperation, people are much more likely to be helpful. Conversely, if you're at odds with someone, they'll likely be unwilling or offer minimal help at best. In the grand scheme of things, forming positive relationships often proves to be the smarter choice, as it opens doors and is a recipe for success in both personal and professional spheres.

It's often a smart move to tuck away our egos for a while and slip into someone else's perspective, like trying on a fresh outfit. Egos have a knack for sneaking into conflicts and conversations, and the result is rarely a pretty picture. We end up with bruised feelings, festering grudges, and the lingering feeling that we need to exact some form of revenge.

I'm not immune to this human tendency; I've fired off emails laced with sarcasm and engaged in conversations that didn't need my two cents, or that could have been more diplomatically handled. It felt like an ego-driven necessity at the time. However, as life adds more notches to your belt and your experience deepens, a revelation dawns: not everything needs to be a battle. In fact, most things aren't, and even when they are, you don't have to engage in the fight.

It's almost astonishing how effortless it can be to flash a smile, nod in agreement, or express a polite disagreement without unleashing a verbal war. This particular vista of perception has been my guide for over the past five years, and it's a curious wonder how such a simple lesson can take so long to learn and yet be so incredibly valuable. It's transformed me into a more composed, self-assured individual and has even enhanced my regard for my fellow travelers on life's winding road. All this is in contrast to the aftermath of conflict, which often left me wallowing in a sea of regret and bitterness.

Taming the ego has been a skill I've honed over time, undoubtedly aided by the wisdom that often comes with age. However, it's also a realization that winning isn't the be-all and end-all; it's the art of effective communication and finding common ground with others that truly matters.

My journey with Jiu-Jitsu has been a noteworthy teacher in this regard. It's a discipline that places a premium on problem-solving rather than relying solely on brute force. Instead of trying to muscle your way out of a situation, it encourages you to navigate challenges with finesse, accentuating the value of strategy and skill over sheer strength. This shift in perspective has not only helped me better understand myself but has also equipped me with valuable tools for navigating the complexities of human interactions. It had a deep impact on how I approach not only martial arts but also many aspects of life, urging me to find solutions and resolutions rather than battles to win.

Choosing to steer clear of unnecessary fights and debates and instead opting for respectful agreement or disagreement without confrontation is a practice that can greatly enrich our lives. Let me illustrate this with a simple example we all encounter: driving and traffic.

Imagine someone cuts you off on the road. Your initial reaction might be to take offense, a response often driven by the ego. However, consider this: that driver could be rushing to the hospital to be by their dying mother's side, late for a crucial meeting, or simply lost in thought. Any of these scenarios are entirely plausible and relatable.

When you view the situation from this perspective, it becomes apparent that the other person isn't necessarily trying to offend you personally. They might be preoccupied, absorbed in their own concerns, or facing a critical situation. Responding with anger or aggression doesn't help the situation; in fact, it exacerbates it. Understanding the possible motives behind others' actions allows us to diffuse tension, practice empathy, and foster a more harmonious coexistence. It's a choice that not only eases our own path but also contributes to a more considerate and compassionate world.

I recommend everyone to seek out a mentor. Why, you ask? Well, picture this: Each of us carries a suitcase of imperfections, much like a quirky collection of travel souvenirs. But what if I told you that we could take our baggage of character flaws, check it at the mentor's counter, and return home with a sleeker, upgraded version of ourselves?

You see, a mentor is like the seasoned traveler who's been to the peaks and troughs, the soul who knows where all the best local secrets are hidden. In their capable hands, we learn to keep our ego in check, like a rambunctious puppy, so it doesn't wreck the neighbor's garden. It's about preserving the sanctity of our personal brand, like a rare, well-aged cheese to be used with pride when the occasion calls. After all, every one of us has our fair share of imperfections, and ensuring that our ego doesn't cast a negative shadow on our outlook and personal brand is crucial.

Finding a mentor holds immense significance, especially when viewed through the lens of masculinity. As men grow older, they often distance themselves from strong relationships, and it's easy to lose sight of the core qualities that define a man – strength, stoicism, and a willingness to lend a helping hand. However, having a mentor who's unafraid to call you out on your nonsense can serve as a grounding force, helping you maintain your focus.

Managing your ego and harnessing it effectively can be greatly aided by building a support network of mentors and peers who have the finesse to broach these matters tactfully as they surface. Finding a seasoned mentor who possesses the kind of wisdom you require can be a game-changer. They have the knack for helping you hit the pause button when you sense your ego surging, and they can guide you in discovering the 'why' behind your ego's activation. Equipped with this understanding, your mentor can then steer you toward strategies for handling your ego, recognizing its triggers, and ensuring it doesn't cast a shadow over your relationships.

It's not a one-size-fits-all deal, though. For various stages of life and a multitude of issues that may arise, you'd do well to gather a team of mentors – a mentor for each chapter and a mentor for each challenge. After all, as the saying goes, it takes a village to tackle ego, character, and the ever-evolving journey of life.

That being said, ego, it turns out, is a double-edged sword. In certain situations, you've got to muster up that self-assuredness and let others know that you're not one to be disrespected or bullied. I, for one, have zero tolerance for bullies and a deep disdain for rudeness in men. It's a line I'm not willing to let anyone cross. But whenever possible, gently putting a leash on that ego is the savvy move.

It's a bit like seasoning in a meal – best used in moderation. Some of history's most iconic figures possessed colossal egos. However, if you dive into the annals of their stories, you'll find that ego often played the villain, leading to their ultimate undoing. You see, ego's unattractive cousin is hubris, and once that sneaky character takes the stage, you start tuning out the voices of mentors and those around you. Suddenly, you become so self-absorbed that you're convinced you know everything. And that, my friends, is the gateway to the land of downfall.

Of course, there are moments where a touch of ego can serve as a shield against disrespect and bullying, helping you maintain your self-respect and draw your boundaries. I recently had an encounter at my house during a UFC fight. An acquaintance, in a bout of bravado, declared, "I don't think jujitsu would work on me." To this, I quipped, "I have a mat room right next door. You can test that assumption at your convenience". It was a verbal mic drop that silenced the naysayer promptly.

However, it's important to recognize that such statements can have ripples of impact, which was exactly what happened in this situation. The impact of my response extended beyond just silencing the initial commenter. It also left an impression on another individual who viewed it as a bold and audacious statement. Later, he confided in me, sharing that my words had made him feel somewhat inadequate. He admitted that he hadn't faced many challenges in the past and didn't carry a particularly large ego.

But a crucial point to bear in mind is that you can't toss around such challenges as idle threats. You must possess the skill and ability to back up your words; otherwise, you're simply writing a check with your mouth that your skills can't cash.

Since the dawn of man, we've witnessed countless instances where people failed to control their egos, often leading to unfortunate consequences for themselves and others. Recently, a man sucker-punched another individual who fell to the ground and ultimately lost his life due to the injury. Now, the person who threw the punch faces an extensive prison sentence, and both families involved will suffer the devastating aftermath of this tragic incident.

These events are reminders that unchecked ego, particularly when it triggers violent actions, can have profound and far-reaching consequences. Ego, by itself, isn't inherently evil. It can be harnessed for positive ends, like standing up to bullies or as a driving force for personal and professional success. However, all too often, it becomes entangled in violent actions, leading to tragedy. Hence, controlling our ego becomes paramount, more than any other task, especially when it threatens to escalate situations into ferocity and tragedy.

Learning to control one's ego and recognizing its duality - both a powerful force and a potentially destructive one - requires time and maturity. Much like a luxurious car, ego can take you to amazing destinations in style and comfort, but if not handled with care, it can veer off course and collide with a retaining wall, causing harm to all on board.

Ego has been a driving force behind countless innovations, the rise of corporations, the development of nations, and the exploration of new frontiers throughout human history. Columbus set sail to discover the New World driven by his ego, just as the exploration of the Arctic Circle was motivated by the ego of many men. Nevertheless, ego can also lead to destructive consequences, such as the annihilation of Troy, which was spurred by ego and resulted in tremendous loss of life.

So, the key takeaway here is to recognize that ego is a potent force, a powerful motivator that can steer you toward success. It can either be a stellar supporting actor or a troublesome scene-stealer. The choice, my friends, is up to us. So, navigate this ego-driven world with a dash of wit, a pinch of wisdom, and a heap of self-awareness, ensuring that your story is one worth telling. Remember, ego is like spice – use it wisely, and you'll savor the flavors of success!

# Chapter 10: Biological Brother

My mother had a soft spot for the name Gary, but my biological father, who made rare appearances in my life, argued against it. He claimed he couldn't bestow that name upon me because he already had a son from a prior relationship who bore the moniker Gary. Hence, I ended up being named after my father instead.

Growing up without a father figure left a noticeable impact on my childhood. It wasn't just the absence of a paternal presence; it was the revolving door of stepfathers, each one seemingly less worthy than the last, that made my upbringing particularly challenging. This tumultuous environment contributed to the sizable chip on my shoulder that I carried with me through those formative years.

More significantly, the absence of a consistent male role model meant I missed out on the indispensable guidance needed to understand what it truly meant to be a man, both in character and conduct. Instead of a mentor's wisdom, I gleaned insights from the pages of magazines and the rugged John Wayne movies – hardly the ideal blueprint for manhood.

Looking back, I can't help but wonder how my life might have been different if I had had a strong, stable role model, someone to emulate and learn from as my son does now. I believe that with such direction, my path might have been more straightforward, leading to success in a more conventional sense. Nevertheless, it's also possible that without the trials and challenges I faced, I might not have developed the same level of resilience and determination that ultimately propelled me towards my current success.

I remember that as a child, there was one passion that ignited my spirit above all else – hunting and fishing. The thought of going on adventures in the wilderness, whether in the craggy landscapes of Alaska or exploring the terrains of Africa, captivated my imagination. The idea of tracking and hunting exotic animals filled my dreams with excitement and wonder.

But amidst these grandiose dreams of exploration, I couldn't escape the reality of my upbringing as the child of a single mother living in trailer parks. Despite the constraints of my circumstances, I harbored a whimsical notion deep within me. I envisioned having an older brother, a globetrotting adventurer who lived a life of daring and exhilarating experiences.

In my mind's eye, he was out there in the world, living an extraordinary and audacious life, undertaking daring exploits that I could only dream of. It was a comforting daydream, a way to escape the limitations of my environment and dream of a life beyond my reach.

One unintended consequence of my mother's choices was the severance of our connection to my father's family. The absence of knowledge that I remain in the dark about the other half of my family tree, the paternal side, frustrated me. I often ponder what influence and support I might have received from that side of the family, especially in terms of a paternal figure. It's a bit like shooting an arrow into the unknown and then trying to paint a bullseye around it. There's a possibility that they could have been wonderful people, but on the flip side, they might have been as problematic as my father's and my mother's families.

Nevertheless, it's hard not to wonder about the cousins, aunts, uncles, and kindred souls who might have been part of my life. Human beings possess an innate yearning to uncover their roots and discover the lineage they are part of. This desire is deeply rooted in our tribal past, where close-knit communities were essential for our survival as a species.

Knowing one's origins and the people with whom they share their heritage is a natural extension of our need for connection and belonging. And so was the case with me as well. Fortunately, I did find a silver lining in knowing a bit about this other side of the family rather later in life.

One day, I was casually scrolling through Facebook, minding my own business, when an email from a certain Anne Marie popped into my inbox. In her message, she boldly declared herself to be my niece and asked, "Hey, are you my uncle?" Now, here's the kicker – I have a pretty unique name, and it turned out we shared the same last name as her grandfather. The odds were definitely in favor of a familial connection. But here's the twist – that email had been floating in cyberspace for a whole year, and Anne Marie seemed to have vanished into thin air. I tried contacting her multiple times, but all attempts to reach her had proven futile.

Fast forward to my adventures on a cruise ship, where I was on a mission to find any and all Anne Maries on the high seas. I did not want to let the opportunity to know the other side of my family slip through the cracks. So, I was in full-on detective mode. After a series of thrilling close calls, I finally struck gold and had a chat with none other than Anne Marie's husband.

Now, here comes the grand reveal – I casually dropped the bombshell on him, saying, "Hey, I think I might be your wife's long-lost uncle." Talk about a plot twist! To my astonishment, he goes, "Hold on a sec, she's walking in the door right now."

And just like that, we had a full-blown family reunion in the making. We swapped stories and info, and Anne Marie played matchmaker to reconnect me with my estranged brother. Ah, the wonders of the digital age and the high seas – you never know where family ties might lead you.

So, I finally got the chance to talk to her and meet my brother in the town of Morris, IL. We gathered for a lovely dinner, complete with good food and even better company. It was a proper family get-together, with my brother, his wife, my niece, and my nephew all present and accounted for. My brother, as it turned out, is a solid guy. He was hanging up his firefighter hat in retirement, residing in Morris, IL. He had a wife, three kids, and a bunch of grandkids – talk about a full house!

Now, here's the twist in the tale. I'd always pictured my long-lost brother as some sort of daring, adventurous soul. In my mind, he was the swashbuckling hero of countless imaginary tales, but reality had a different tale to tell. He was leading a quieter, more down-to-earth life.

The humorous thing is that all those years, I had painted this vivid mental picture of him as a globetrotting adventurer, leaping from one thrilling escapade to another. But when we finally crossed paths, reality came crashing down. He was, well, exactly the opposite of the adventurous hero I'd conjured up in my mind. In fact, he was a thoroughly decent, middle-class fellow. His life appeared normal, and I couldn't help but see it as somewhat uneventful. It was the epitome of a middle-class existence, which I had somehow managed to label as 'boring.' I guess our imaginations often have a penchant for adding a bit more spice than reality allows.

My brother and I couldn't be more different if we tried. For starters, he's got a solid nine years on me and is a bit on the burly side with dark hair, while I seem to have inherited my mother's genes, standing tall, slim, and in pretty good shape.

Our differences go beyond appearances, though. Our personalities are like night and day; he's the quiet, introverted type, while I'm the life of the party, always the outgoing one. It's like we were cut from entirely different molds. Looking back, I had totally mixed up the reel with the real. He hadn't been off chasing adrenaline-pumping adventures; instead, he was living a content, grounded life. And honestly, there's absolutely nothing wrong with that. I just had been projecting my own desires onto his life, with no reason to assume he was anything but true to himself. It was a reminder that sometimes, our expectations don't quite match up with reality, and that's okay. Lesson learned - we should be understanding and accepting of the reality of our loved ones' lives rather than imposing our own expectations upon them.

The catch is that all those audacious dreams and aspirations I'd projected onto him? Turns out, I ended up fulfilling them myself. I have circled the globe, served as a US paratrooper, earned a Brazilian Jiu-Jitsu black belt, and even snagged an MBA, just to name a few achievements. Life has a funny way of having the last laugh, doesn't it?

It's pretty wild how a kid's imagination can take flight, especially when you're growing up in a unique set of circumstances. For me, not having a father figure or an older brother paved the way for some interesting expectations. In retrospect, I can see how the absence of a strong male influence left me to my own devices. There was no one around to ground me or give me a nudge in the right direction. Everything began to change when I took a critical step by joining the army. It was a turning point that provided a taste of success, and it opened the door to a world of opportunities.

That's when it hit me – I could do anything I put my mind to. It was a game-changer, the point where my journey really took off. So, in a way, I owe my early dreams and my later triumphs to the power of a young kid's imagination and the prospects that life tossed my way.

Again, not graduating high school could've easily been a roadblock for me that led to failure. But I decided to take that detour and join the army instead. Little did I know that this twist in the plot would become a transformative factor.

Once I stepped into the military world, that's when things really started to click. My confidence, abilities, and resilience skyrocketed. As I mentioned earlier, I was part of the 101st Airborne Division and the 5th Special Forces Group. The sheer number of awards and accolades that came my way was mind-boggling.

Those military experiences were like fuel for my ambition. They pushed me to earn my undergraduate degree, and eventually, I even earned myself an MBA. But that's not all. I became scuba certified, rocked the airborne and air assault qualifications, and powered through some of the toughest army schools you can imagine. Who would've thought that a high school hiccup could lead to such a dynamic journey? Life's full of surprises!

We all enter the world with preconceived notions, and it's an inevitable part of life. But I've come to understand that these perceptions can either work as constraints or stepping stones, depending on how we choose to handle them. The key? Education.

By educating yourself and digging into these notions, whether they're your own or those you hold toward others, you start to grasp that you can't truly know if they're accurate until you've dived headfirst into the matter. It's a reminder that there's always more to the story than meets the eye.

Resilience, especially in the face of adversity, is an invaluable gift, and I believe it's something we should instill in our children, sons in particular. The world, despite the privileges we enjoy in this country, can be an extremely tough place. Life has a knack for throwing curveballs our way, but it's the ability to bounce back and move forward with gritty determination that really counts.

I often share a piece of advice with everyone: never sit by the side of the road for too long because, eventually, you've got to pick yourself up and keep moving forward. Resilience is the fuel that powers that journey. It's the catalyst for personal growth, not just physically but mentally as well. So, pass that resilience on to the next generation to guarantee they're well-equipped for the challenges of life.

I don't value a normal, fulfilling life. Who would ever want a 'normal' life when the world is teeming with a smorgasbord of contests and adventures waiting to be devoured? Normal can be as exciting as watching paint dry. Life's an epic rollercoaster ride, and there's no fun in standing in line for the kiddie coaster.

A man, in my view, needs to have strong personal values and aspirations that drive him forward. I'm not talking about world domination or inventing the next big thing like the iPhone, though that'd be cool, too. I am talking about leading a life that's rich, fulfilled, and far from ordinary. After all, who doesn't want to look back at their life and have a thrilling story to tell? Those who settle for mediocrity and a lack of motivation are missing out on the adventure of a lifetime.

Now, it's worth noting that while we need our share of go-getters and adventurers, we also require the steady presence of those who are content with the ordinary. It's a world of contrasting roles that keep the balance in check.

I love sharing this with everyone – I've overachieved in life, and that's a fact. Given my upbringing, you could say there were slim expectations for me to be anything other than your typical trailer park kid, but I've come a long way since then. In my rearview mirror, I see a trail of achievements and personal growth, and it fills me with immense pride. Yet, it's all wrapped in a generous layer of humility because, let's be real, things could have taken a wrong turn at any moment.

Goal-setting is what it takes - having aspirations, being driven, and going after what you want with a kind of hunger is the fire you need to have. However, the key is setting realistic goals. As much as we'd all love to see a 5-foot-5 woman in the NBA, that's probably stretching the bounds of reality a bit too far.

The secret sauce is in starting with small, achievable goals. Get those under your belt, build up that momentum, and then keep leveling up. Construct a staircase to your dreams — one step at a time, one goal at a time. It's a recipe for success and progress that makes every win taste that much sweeter. Find that sweet spot between realism and ambition. We need goals that are not only attainable but also a bit of a stretch, ones that push us out of our comfort zones. That's where the magic happens, where real growth and transformation occur.

Once you start achieving those goals, it's like a domino effect. You can build on them, set new goals, and keep expanding your horizons. It's the very technique for building resilience and developing a strong, unshakable character. So, let's keep setting those goals and watching our lives transform one achievement at a time.

# Chapter 11: Continuing to Grow and Push the Envelope

In life, there's one thread I hold dearer than a pot of gold – the zeal for perpetual learning and unbridled growth. I've never aspired to live a pedestrian existence; instead, I've harbored a keen desire to be that individual who defies the gravitational pull of stagnation.

I've often quipped, much to the amusement (or bewilderment) of those around me, that if I ever find myself reigning supreme as the oracle of wisdom in any given room, it's a sign I've inadvertently wandered into the wrong room altogether. I mean, let's face it: being the brightest bulb in the chandelier is an overrated status. It's akin to winning a race with snails – sure, you're ahead, but where's the thrill?

Contrast that with some folks in my family who, bless their hearts, seem to have an avid thirst for being perpetually right. They crave omniscience like it's going out of style. Now, call me a rebel, but I firmly believe that's the fastest route to intellectual fossilization. I mean, think about it – if you're already the walking, talking Encyclopedia Britannica, when do you find time to add new chapters? If you know everything, what can you learn?

I relish the discomfort of not knowing something. It's the sweet spot where curiosity takes the wheel, and the joy of discovery becomes an exhilarating road trip. Sometimes, I might be in a state of blissful ignorance because I'm simply making room for a new nugget of knowledge to waltz in and make itself at home.

Surrounded by the brilliance of high-performance consultants and individuals, I developed an appreciation for learning. My curiosity has always driven me to explore a multitude of diverse and disparate topics. And so, breaking free from the shackles of needing to be always right and all-knowing became a pivotal milestone in my personal growth journey. It struck me that my desire to always be right was, ironically, impeding my own development. Reading a bunch of books and reflecting on my own maturity helped me realize that the less I claimed to know, the more I could actually learn and absorb new insights.

This epiphany led me to consciously shift my approach - to become an avid listener, to seek understanding, and to embrace the humility that comes with acknowledging the vast expanse of what I didn't know.

This shift not only fueled my personal growth but also helped me connect with people. It turns out that people like talking about themselves, and they appreciate someone who listens. Everyone, it seems, revels in the sound of their own narrative. Also, everyone wants to feel heard and understood, and I found that's the real key to building relationships.

I thrive on pushing my limits, both physically and mentally, and it's a mantra I passionately share with those around me. I refuse to be the person idly scrolling through social media while others live out their adventures—I'd much rather be out there creating my own.

The drive to push my limits stems from a constant desire for improvement and a quest to defy the effects of time and fend off the relentless march of Father Time. I take pride in striving to surpass my contemporaries in every aspect, whether it's physical prowess or mental acuity. I've made it a personal mission to constantly make myself better, which is a commitment to evolve and outpace the expectations placed on me, both by others and, more importantly, by myself.

It's not about competition with others; rather, it's a competition with my own potential. The joy lies not just in the victory but in the process of continuous refinement. After all, life's an adventure, and I plan on living it on the frontlines, not as a spectator.

I recall the time when my wife and I visited the former prison on Alcatraz Island in San Francisco. As we gazed across the bay at the city's skyline, I casually mentioned that I could "make that swim." My wife, ever the skeptic, threw down the challenge, saying, "Why don't you then?" And just like that, the idea of conquering the Alcatraz to San Francisco Bay swim was born.

Undeterred, I dove into months of rigorous training at my local pool, carving out time every other day to prepare for this ambitious endeavor. However, life had other plans. The first year was marred by an unexpected elbow injury, which was a setback that forced me to pause my training. The following year, just as I geared up for the swim, COVID-19 intervened, putting my plans on hold.

Yet, regardless of these hurdles, I maintained a firm commitment. Every morning at 5:30 AM, come rain or shine, I plunged into the pool, resolute to conquer the challenges that stood between me and the cold waters of the bay.

Despite the setbacks of injury and dealing with COVID-19, I maintained a laser focus on my training, determined to ensure that I put in the necessary work for success. In 2021, alongside an old army buddy, I finally faced the daunting Alcatraz swim. Sharing the experience with my army buddy added an extra layer of enjoyment. Even though we hadn't seen each other for a couple of years, the bond forged in the military ensured that army friends remained friends forever.

The nerves were intense as we prepared to plunge into the daunting waters. The moment I entered the 60-degree water, the reality hit – my wet suit felt like a second skin, so tight that I had to unzip it as I powered through the waves. For an hour and a half, I navigated the dark, tannic waters, aware of the lurking mysteries beneath – sharks, octopuses, and other creatures ready for a meal.

Emerging from the bay, my legs wobbly, I could barely stand. Yet, pride surged within me. At 55, against all odds, I had conquered the formidable Alcatraz swim. It's a Spartan lifestyle I relish – taking on discomfort, denying myself ease, and achieving feats that defy societal expectations. After all, not many people get on board such adventures, especially in their mid-50s. It's the thrill of the challenge and the sweet taste of victory that makes it all worthwhile.

Post-swim, we celebrated with a meal and a few drinks. The evening became a perfect opportunity to catch up, share stories, and reminisce about the good old days. It reaffirmed the belief that some friendships are timeless, and the shared triumph of conquering the challenging swim created memories that will last a lifetime.

\*\*\*

The pages of my life in this book, as you can tell by now, state a tale of feats, from putting on the military uniform without a high school diploma to earning a master's degree and the exhilaration of being a paratrooper, skydiver, and scuba diver. It's been a journey marked by blessings and the sweet nectar of fulfillment.

Back in the early days, fortune smiled upon me when a recruiter extended a helping hand, making a contract that allowed me to join the army despite lacking a high school education. Though he received no credit for my enlistment, he secured me a spot, setting the stage for the unfolding chapters of my unconventional life.

Admittedly, my initial stint as a soldier was average; I was, at best, a mediocre servicemember. However, fate had grander plans for me. It was when I found myself stationed in the illustrious 101st Airborne Division that my military journey truly soared to new heights. As I stated earlier, the division's storied history served as a catalyst, igniting a sense of purpose within me and propelling me toward elite status. The 101st Airborne Division was more than just a duty station; it was a canvas upon which I painted the vivid colors of my potential.

Becoming a paratrooper, skydiver, and scuba diver were not just checkboxes on a bucket list; they were natural extensions of my audacious personality. I've always sought to tread where others dared not since I find joy in the quest for the extraordinary. I'd dare anyone to find another individual who has taken on all three roles and conquered the three – the sky, the sea, and the earth below.

Another feather in my cap is my foray into Brazilian Jiu-Jitsu in 2013. The allure of BJJ always tickled my fancy, and when my son hopped on the training bandwagon, I thought, "Why not join the fun?" I kicked off this martial arts adventure at the ripe age of 47 – a decision some might call audacious, but I call it seizing the moment.

For those of you who might not know, BJJ is not a Sunday stroll in the park; it's a full-on body workout that throws wrestling, judo, and grappling into a blender. It's the kind of sport that makes even the most seasoned athletes pause and question their life choices. Every class feels like a crash course in pushing your physical limits. But, well, where's the fun without a bit of challenge, right? Truth be told, many people throw in the towel right after snagging their blue belts.

Statistically speaking, less than 1% of initiates make it to the coveted black belt level. It's the Everest of martial arts, and I decided to plant my flag at the summit.

Ten years, a few battle scars, and a truckload of resilience later, I proudly stand among the mythical 1% who've ascended to the black belt echelon. It's been a journey filled with injuries, triumphs, and a whole lot of sweat, but achieving that black belt is a badge of honor I wear with a grin wider than a Cheshire cat.

Beyond the joy it's brought to my life, BJJ has gifted me a camaraderie akin to the tight-knit bonds I forged in the military. Call me sentimental, but it's more than a sport; it's a journey that has defined the contours of my pride and made me a card-carrying member of the elite 1%.

I competed across multiple countries against a diverse array of opponents, which became a hallmark of my journey in Brazilian Jiu-Jitsu. With over 20 International Brazilian Jiu-Jitsu Federation events under my belt, I've clinched my fair share of gold, silver, and bronze medals. Currently, I find immense pride and joy in imparting the art of BJJ to a dedicated group of students at my academy.

Every competition, every opponent, and every country brought me not just closer to the sport but also closer to my fellow warriors on the mat. Jiu-Jitsu is a unique brand of intimate combat, forging bonds that go beyond mere camaraderie – it's a man-to-man struggle, a test of skill and willpower to determine who will submit and who will emerge victorious. It's a special breed that not only takes up the challenge of starting Jiu-Jitsu but persists in donning the coveted black belt.

In BJJ, friendships aren't just made; they are molded through the shared experiences of grappling and striving for mastery. I've got buddies scattered across the globe and a global network of connections, all thanks to the community fostered by Brazilian Jiu-Jitsu. It's a sport, but more than that, I believe it's a lifestyle that binds us together, transcending borders and creating bonds that endure far beyond the mat.

I personally believe that BJJ is the maestro of problem-solving, honing your focus exclusively on the immediate challenge at hand while magically evaporating any other concerns that might clutter your mind. Picture this: a 200-pound human sitting on your chest – suddenly, work, relationships, and dinner plans vanish. Your entire mental landscape is dedicated to one singular task: figuring out how to get this guy off you.

But here's the kicker: when you're on the offensive, working to submit your opponent, they're not exactly handing it to you on a silver platter. Nope, you've got to work that problem too. It thrusts you directly into the thick of the moment, demanding your utmost focus, or else face the consequences.

Forget work problems, social dilemmas, or relationship drama – in the world of BJJ, your mental real estate is reserved solely for the task of either avoiding submission or achieving it. And for the uninitiated, submitting means making your opponent tap out. A tap is their way of saying, "Okay, you got me,' basically saying 'I yield.' It's the safe way to train without the risk of being choked out, or limbs snapped like twigs.

These problem-solving skills aren't confined to the mat. Brazilian Jujitsu enthusiasts carry this mental clarity into their personal and professional lives. The ability to tackle challenges one move at a time to stay focused in the chaos becomes a blueprint for success beyond the mat. Brazilian Jiu-Jitsu is a philosophy and mindset that sharpens the blade of problem-solving, making practitioners adept at navigating the complexities of life itself, whether in a sparring match or the boardroom.

I have personally noticed that training in BJJ has bestowed upon me a Zen-like calmness. I sometimes feel that I have an enhanced sense of relaxation and a sharpened focus that spills over into both my professional and personal spheres. Now, let's be clear – choking out colleagues or employees isn't on the agenda, but the fundamental principles of relaxation and focused problem-solving certainly are.

BJJ has become my secret sauce for maintaining composure in the face of conflicts, both at work and in my personal life. It's a lesson in working towards a solution rather than getting bogged down by emotions or overthinking. Tension is the enemy; it drains your energy, leaving you vulnerable. The same holds true in life – whether it's a professional setback or a personal conflict, being overly upset or overthinking rarely solves the issue. The key, as I've come to learn, is to work the problem.

When you've got an opponent your size hell-bent on submitting you, the key is focus and relaxation. Tensing up leads to fatigue, and in the world of BJJ, fatigue equals defeat. This lesson translates seamlessly to life off the mat – stay focused, stay relaxed, and tackle problems head-on. It's a practical philosophy that's far more effective than succumbing to stress or letting emotions run wild. The mat is a microcosm of life's challenges, and the lessons learned there ripple into every aspect of my existence.

So, while I won't be employing a rear-naked choke on my coworkers anytime soon, I will undoubtedly leverage the cool-headed, problem-solving mindset that BJJ has instilled in me.

As I touched upon in the previous chapter, BJJ is a masterclass in humility. The saying in our BJJ community,

"The mats don't lie," encapsulates this perfectly. Regardless of your appearance or how fast, big, or strong you may seem, the mat has a knack for revealing your weaknesses. It's an honest mirror reflecting your flexibility, cardio endurance, and strength. There's no room for deception on the mat, and it demands respect for everyone, regardless of their outward appearance.

I realized that in BJJ, those who may seem unassuming, weak, or small can possess a deadly skill set. It's a reminder that looks can be deceiving; someone may appear helpless, but their mastery of technique can turn the tables in an instant. Thus, the philosophy is simple: treat everyone with respect, acknowledging and appreciating their unique skill set.

Moreover, the impact of BJJ isn't confined to the gym. It's an art that infiltrates daily life, acting as a balm for the irritations that might trigger road rage or inflame anger. The practice sharpens self-awareness, alerting you when tension creeps in and guiding you back to a relaxed state. It's a journey that reshapes not just your physical abilities but your mental and emotional responses, fostering a mindset grounded in respect, humility, and a keen awareness of one's own vulnerabilities.

The knowledge that I hold the capability to handle myself in physical confrontations brings about calmness. It acts as a deterrent against engaging in street fights fueled by ego. Instead of surrendering to the temptation of proving oneself through aggression, the realization that I can walk away from confrontations becomes a source of empowerment.

When faced with insults or provocations, the awareness of my martial arts training serves as a shield against the potential harm of ego-driven conflicts. The ability to discern that someone posing verbal threats lacks the capacity to back them up diminishes the significance of their words. In essence, it renders insults and threats meaningless unless accompanied by genuine skill and intent.

Having the knowledge that I could potentially overpower most individuals with my bare hands provides restraint. It instills a conscious choice to avoid unnecessary fights, recognizing that engaging in conflict with those who lack real threat is not a display of strength but rather an act of insecurity. As a trained martial artist, the focus isn't on showcasing prowess; it's on maintaining composure and using skills judiciously.

In essence, the wisdom gained from martial arts extends beyond physical prowess to a deeper understanding of the psychology behind conflicts. It highlights the pointlessness of engaging in battles driven by insecurity and bravado. Rather than seeking validation through physical altercations, the martial artist's path is one of measured self-assurance, where the true victory lies in the ability to walk away, untouched by the provocations of those who may bark but lack the bite to back it up.

*** 

Life's challenges have been my sculptor, molding me into the person I am today. They've acted as my personal ego-buster, chiseling away at any inflated sense of self-importance and generously sprinkling humility in its place. It's like life's way of saying, "Hey, everyone's got their own wild journey, and yours doesn't come with a roadmap. Embrace the detours!"

Now, enduring both physical and mental challenges throughout the years has been the crucible for forging my grit. Grit, my friend, is not something you pick up at the corner store; it's a bespoke creation crafted through hardship and diligently refined like a well-crafted piece of literature. I take particular joy in doing things that are harder than teaching a cat to tap dance because, well, when emergencies come knocking, they find me casually sipping tea because I've already conquered the hard stuff.

Here's my sage advice: keep pumping those muscles physically, expand those brain folds mentally, and absorb knowledge like a sponge at a water park. Oh, and throw some jujitsu into the mix! Now, I'm not just telling you to casually stroll through life; no, I mean wrestle with the tough stuff. Fight against the currents, climb the steepest mental mountains, and flex those resilience muscles. Life's a perpetual struggle, my friend, and we might as well make it a stylish, jujitsu-infused tango with the challenging bits.

Let's wrap up this chapter with a truth bomb: life is one tough cookie. Staying in top-notch shape? That's hard. Acquiring a wealth of knowledge? Equally hard. Remaining humble? Yep, you guessed it, still hard. Now, flip the coin. Being out of shape? Hard. Moving at a snail's pace? Also hard. Embracing a lack of knowledge? Oh, you better believe that's hard, too. Life is hard, my friend. But here's the thing – you get to choose your hard.

My unsolicited advice is to seek out challenges that make you sweat both physically and mentally. Dive headfirst into the deep end of hard things, and don't you dare throw in the towel. Keep training, keep pushing, and you'll emerge from the crucible with resiliency and grit – the kind that's built through sweat and struggle.

Now, imagine for a moment: life taps you on the shoulder one day, urging you to use that finely tuned body of yours to save someone – maybe your own family, a friend, or even a total stranger. Can you imagine saying, "Sorry folks, I didn't train because I was feeling a bit lazy"? That's a tough pill to swallow. Or how about being stranded in the vast ocean, desperately wishing you'd bothered to learn to swim? Life's risky, no doubt, but you can stack the odds in your favor by embracing the challenge of hard things.

So, choose your hard wisely, my friend. Train, grow, and make life's hurdles a little less daunting. Because, in the grand performance of existence, you want to be the one gracefully leaping over the obstacles, not stumbling over them.

# Chapter 12: The Mosaic of Life

As I stand here at 57, looking back at the mosaic of my life, it feels complete. If my time on this earthly stage were to end tomorrow, I'd exit with a remarkably short list of regrets. After all, it's the things we haven't done that haunt us, not the daring adventures we've embraced. While there are still many chapters I wish to write, I find contentment in the narrative so far. The last thing I'd ever want is to be a forgettable footnote.

The man you see today is a content one. I've scaled the peaks of overachievement, forging a path that's led to a centered and stable existence. It's not that I'm done achieving - oh no, there's always more I want to conquer. Professionally, I've bopped through two careers and now find myself waltzing into a third, with success applauding my endeavors. In my professional circle, I've become a trusted figure, with colleagues seeking advice and networking opportunities.

On the personal front, being happily married to the same incredible woman for 35 years has been my greatest blessing. All my successes wear her fingerprints just as much as mine. Together, we've nurtured a son who's not just a chip off the old block but a successful consultant carving out his own narrative. He graduated from the same master's program that once claimed my focus, and now, he's crafting a tale uniquely his own.

So, as I am penning the last few pages of this autobiography, I relish the contentment of a life well-lived, in my opinion, the thrill of new achievements waiting on the skyline and the joy of watching my family members write their own compelling stories. The journey may not be over, but darn, it has been one captivating ride so far.

Reflecting on the journey, it's almost comical. I had distant family members growing up in what some might call 'normal' households - two parents, middle-class comfort. To society, they might have been middle class, but to me, that was wealth beyond imagination. Here I was, the son of a single mother with no real male guidance, barely scraping by. Growing up poor, skinny, and malnourished, without a father figure, surviving seemed like a miracle, let alone thriving. It's a tough hand to deal with, especially as a male, but it gifted me something money couldn't buy: grit.

The disadvantages I faced became the catalyst for a relentless work ethic. It forged a toughness that's not easily built. I often think of it as a secret weapon, an invisible armor that made me work harder than those who had it easier. If I could give advice to every man out there, especially fathers, it would be this: instill grit and toughness in your children, particularly your boys.

Despite societal norms and the complexities of our woke world, it's the men who will stand guard, keep the wolf at bay, and throw themselves into the breach when needed. Now, let me be clear: I am not trying to promote or encourage violence in any form but simply trying to emphasize that grit, fortitude, and a willingness to stand up when the chips are down are the very qualities that safeguard our nation.

Even though society has certain expectations about how men and women should behave, one thing that's often expected of men is to be like protectors. This means they're seen as the ones who should watch out for potential problems and step up when things get tough. In a community or a family, men are the ones looked at to keep everyone safe from challenges or difficulties, just like guards keeping watch for any trouble. This responsibility isn't just about sticking to old-fashioned ideas; it's about recognizing that men can be strong and reliable figures who help everyone around them. So, when people say men stand guard, they mean they're expected to be dependable and ready to face whatever comes their way, making sure things stay safe and secure.

In a world that sometimes forgets the value of resilience and toughness, fathers play a crucial role in shaping individuals who can weather life's storms. It's a call to arms, not just for survival but for thriving in the face of adversity. Because let's face it, if our men lack grit, fortitude, and a willingness to get their hands dirty, our country might as well be waving the white flag. Without a foundation of grit, a nation risks losing its essence and its ability to stand tall against the challenges that come its way. In the end, it's not the fittest who triumph but the grittiest.

In the early chapters, I found myself fumbling through romance, not exactly a maestro when it came to success with the fairer sex. Couple that with the backdrop of extreme poverty, a frame that resembled a living skeleton, and a diet that knew nothing of nourishment - those were the ingredients for a cocktail of insecurity in my youth. Yet, adversity, my ever-present companion, wasn't content with just tagging along; it decided to fuel my internal fire.

Leaving high school was like escaping a poorly scripted teen drama, and joining the army was my ticket to a real-life action movie. The initial chapters might have been a bit shaky, but they laid the foundation for the resilient spirit that defines me today. The chip on my shoulder, born from those early insecurities, became a driving force, propelling me to work tirelessly.

Fast forward to the business world, where I've become the CEO of my own storyline. It's not just a journey; it's a transformation – physically, mentally, emotionally – a trilogy of self-development that would put any superhero origin story to shame. I now wear the highlight reel of accomplishments like a badge of honor. First up, I served in the United States military as a paratrooper. Then, took a plunge into the depths of the ocean as a certified scuba diver and then graduated with an MBA, proving that the kid with the chip on his shoulder could not only compete but excel in the academic arena. And, of course, let's not forget the Brazilian Jiu-Jitsu black belt – a journey that involved blood, sweat, and the occasional mat burn. All these milestones are etched with pride.

Yet, amidst these triumphs, perhaps the most monumental feat is a 35-year marriage that stands as a testament to love, commitment, and weathering life's storms together. Together with my wife, we not only made a successful union but raised a fine young man who's a genuinely good human being.

Now, let's talk about the unfortunate reality check: not everyone upgrades from a bicycle to a sleek sports car; some end up hitchhiking or stuck on a perpetual bus route. It's a shame, really. I occasionally peek back at my high school days, and I'm astounded by those who still treat it like their personal highlight reel. If that were my peak, I might have retired from life by now. But no, I've been on a rollercoaster of achievements, and I'm convinced the real showstopper is yet to hit the stage.

While some are stuck on the nostalgia train, I'm busy preparing for the grand finale. Why settle for a cozy spot on the couch when you can have a front-row seat to the spectacular fireworks of personal growth? I personally believe that the best chapters of my life are still in the editing room, getting polished for an epic release.

If there is one golden nugget of wisdom I've unearthed from my journey, it is the alchemy of success. It is crafted by the hands of those willing to put in the extra effort, to train a bit harder and to persist when others may falter. This philosophy, a cornerstone of my journey, has proven to be the magic wand that transforms aspirations into reality. By cranking up the volume of hard work just a bit more than the average Joe, you unlock a treasure trove of possibilities. It's the difference between a standard-issue life and one cranked up to eleven. By outworking the ordinary, one can extract extraordinary rewards from life.

Like many, I, too, once clung to the familiar, hesitant to tread the unpredictable terrain of transformation and feared change. But as I glance over my shoulder at life's highlight reel, the transformative moments, both the hits and the misses, stand out like stars in the night sky.

Let's start with the bold move of quitting high school – a decision that raised eyebrows but, looking back, unfolded into a masterclass in resilience. Then came the grand entrance into military life, a career in camouflage that painted my life with a palette of discipline and achievement. A plot twist that brought my beautiful wife into the picture, creating a love story that even Hollywood might envy.

But the show didn't end there; oh no, it just took an intermission. Transitioning out of the military, I strapped on my academic armor and marched into Graduate School, which proved to be a journey that told me that I could conquer civilian life with the same fervor as a soldier navigating the battlefield. So, while change may wear the cloak of uncertainty, my narrative attests that within its folds lie the threads of growth, resilience, and unexpected blessings.

When I was at my first duty station, I wore the cloak of a rebel, a bit of a thug without a mentor. Fighting and insubordination were practically my calling cards, and the army brass was contemplating showing me the exit door. Direction? that was as elusive as a pot of gold at the end of a rainbow.

However, Fort Campbell became the turning point. It was there, amidst the rigors and expectations, that I caught sight of a glimmer of potential success if I rolled up my sleeves and put in the work. A fresh start, a clean slate where I could shed the labels of rebel and nonconformist.

Leaving the military enclave at the tender age of 34, armed with a wife, three kids, and a glaring lack of civilian experience, was nothing short of a nerve-wracking endeavor. The abyss of uncertainty yawned before me, and the prospect was, let's be honest, downright scary. But despite the fear, there was a quiet confidence brewing within me – a belief that I could bet on myself.

Transitioning from the army to the mysterious realm of Graduate School was like stepping into the unknown. Could I hold my own against these brainiacs who seemed to have it all figured out? Well, surprise, surprise – not only did I hold my own, but I aced the challenge. It was my golden ticket to transitioning into the world of consulting, where success has been my faithful companion.

Never one to hand out or ask for unearned favors, I set out on a civilian career that would prove to be the jackpot for my family and me. Success, in its multifaceted glory, flowed into our lives – financially and physically. My career choices became the source that allowed my wife and son to taste the richness of life beyond their wildest dreams. We traversed almost every continent, soaking in the diversity of our world.

Joining the army was a support that pulled me out of the clutches of poverty, handed me the keys to undergraduate education, and set me on a trajectory toward success. Military accomplishments and accolades adorned my professional journey. They weren't just tokens; they were the confidence boosters I needed to steer through the civilian life with the assurance that success was not just a possibility but an inevitability.

*** 

If I talk about family bonds, the linchpin is undeniably my wife. Her staunch support has been the backbone of our relationship. She is my confidant and, in my own little world, the consiglieri of our family.

Through the ebb and flow of life, she has stood by my side, globe-trotting to some of the most remote corners of the planet. Not just a passenger, she's been the co-pilot, directing the twists and turns with grace. Whenever I felt stuck in a job that didn't spark joy, she stood by me, cheering on my decision to switch gears and supporting my decisions to pivot and seek fulfillment elsewhere.

Our dynamic is a two-way street. While she leans on me to support her and our children, it's reciprocated with an unspoken trust that has withstood the tests of time. Her support is the entire foundation upon which our family's adventures and aspirations are built. She's not just my better half; she's the secret ingredient that adds flavor to my journey, making every step, whether in the bustling city or the quiet remoteness of the world, an enriching experience.

I owe a tremendous amount to my wife. I know she will be reading this very soon, so I want to put it out there into the pages of this book to be imprinted for a lifetime: *Donna, you are my everything, and I wouldn't be remotely close to where I am today without you. I love you, and you are the absolute best thing that has ever happened to me.*

One meaningful piece of advice I would give to everyone: lay the groundwork with mutual respect and love. However, don't let the warmth of affection blind you to the possibility of others taking advantage. It's a cautionary note I've observed in the relationships of close friends.

In relationships, be generous with your giving. Shower love, wisdom, help, and advice freely, but do it without expecting anything in return. Genuine giving isn't a transaction; it's a selfless art that adds depth to the canvas of any relationship. So, my fellows, build on love, sprinkle it with respect, and let your generosity flow like a river, free from the expectations of reciprocation. That is the essence of true connection.

Always remember that your life story is an ongoing journey - always evolving. Regardless of your age or where you currently find yourself, the ability to mold the person you aspire to be remains at your fingertips. My advice is simple: dedicating a bit more effort each day can lead to a better life. You might not become the next Warren Buffett, Steve Jobs, or Elon Musk, but you'll certainly be a better version of yourself than you were yesterday.

Commit to the process, dedicate yourself to continuous learning, and persistently pursue your goals. This isn't just about working hard; it's about investing in your own improvement. The capacity is clear – your life is poised to become richer, more fulfilling, and undoubtedly better. The choice is yours, so make the right one and take action. Your journey to a better life begins with a simple decision to get after it.

\*\*\*

To all those who've invested their time, whether through purchase, sneak peek, or borrowed glances at these pages, my heartfelt gratitude. It's a project born out of passion and is a labor of love, a collection of experiences, and I genuinely hope it radiates positivity for you. Within these pages lie nuggets of wisdom gleaned from the sweat and toil of hard work, lessons that I hope you can carry forward to enrich your own journey.

My expedition is far from over; I anticipate it to be an adventure with an open-ended storyline, and I envision it continuing for a long, long time. However, I encourage you to envision your life's journey with a sense of contentment. Understandably, not every dream may materialize, as life has its own script. But, by putting one foot in front of the other, maintaining focus, and embracing discipline, you'll find that you can sculpt a life filled with accomplishments and satisfaction. These qualities, I believe, are the compass points for a more fulfilling life.

So, let this be more than just a read; let it be a catalyst for you to get moving, stay focused, and infuse discipline into your pursuits. Life may not unfold precisely as planned, for none of us gets to check off every box on our wish list. Yet, through action, focus, and discipline, you will undoubtedly accomplish some of those dreams.

Reflecting on my journey, I can proudly say that I've not only met but exceeded every expectation I set for myself. What's even more satisfying is surpassing the expectations that others, who once envisioned a different path for me, had placed upon me during my youth. Against the odds and stereotypes, I defied the prospect of becoming a "trailer park failure" and not amounting to much. Luck played its part, and I made some pivotal choices that paved the way for my success today.

However, the true driving force behind my journey is a firm self-belief. For over 50 years, I've subjected myself to challenges, often tasting success but always persisting. The key has been a resolute faith in my capabilities. The experiences shared in this manuscript book are proof of the power of self-belief and the impact it can have on one's life.

As you reach the end of these pages, I want to extend my sincere thanks again for joining me on this literary adventure. I hope my story has resonated with you, even if in a small way. May it serve as a reminder that your journey is yours to mold, and with belief, tenacity, and dust of luck, you can shape a destiny that exceeds even your loftiest aspirations. Here's to your success, deserving and abundant. May your path be filled with accomplishments and fulfillment. Cheers to the adventure that lies ahead, and may the story of your life continue to unfold with brilliance and purpose!

*Exciting news is on the horizon! The journey doesn't end here; it takes a new turn as I stand on the brink of launching a new venture. In this next chapter, I'm thrilled to announce that I'll be monetizing my experience as a professional executive coach and keynote speaker. If curiosity has sparked within you, and you're eager to discover more about this venture, hop on the digital express and visit www.kenaibusinesssolutions.com. The adventure continues, and I'm excited to have you join me in this next phase of growth and exploration.*

www.ingramcontent.com/pod-product-compliance
Lightning Source LLC
Chambersburg PA
CBHW051201120626
46547CB00012B/1162